P9-DIB-047

If you are divorcing, one of the best things you can do for your children is to read this book. Children need two involved, well-functioning parents, but this is hard for parents to do without help. Green and Burrett's little book provides all the advice, help, and encouragement you need. A treasure trove of ideas and wisdom.

Sanford L. Braver, PhD, author of
Divorced Dads: Shattering the Myth

Shared Parenting is eminently readable, chock filled with practical suggestions about how to examine your own assumptions and reactions, consider your ex-spouse's, and keep your children at the heart of every decision. The authors have clearly been around the block a few times and have listened carefully to the feelings and concerns of moms, dads, and children.

Marsha Kline Pruett, PhD, MSL, coauthor of *Partnership Parenting: How Men and Women Parent Differently—and How It Can Help Your Kids and Your Marriage*

Shared Parenting is a blueprint for divorcing parents to use as they try to figure out the next steps of being parents. It is full of helpful hints, probing questions and answers, and is highly readable and engaging. It serves as a tremendously useful guide to rebuilding relationships post-divorce. Any parent going through a divorce can learn from it.

Shared Parenting encourages mothers and fathers to refocus their attention away from the negatives of divorce toward the positives of co-parenting, with the clear focus on the best interests of the children. This book is highly useful in asking and answering the questions all parents must consider as they develop a new family plan and dynamic to ensure that the children do not lose either parent and that their children's needs are paramount.

Jody Mosten, PhD, clinical psychologist, Los Angeles

This book should be compulsory reading for all separating parents. We know children cope best with a family breakup when their parents work together to share their care. But it isn't easy. Burrett and Green have the experience and knowledge to provide practical advice that gives parents a very valuable blueprint for making it happen.

Bettina Arndt, social commentator in Sydney

An eminently practical and sensible guide that helps parents keep their children's needs front and center while working out the details of post-divorce life. This book provides essential information in a user-friendly format. Read this book, apply its advice, and you will give your children an enormous advantage in coping with separation and divorce.

Dr. Richard A. Warshak, Clinical Professor, University of Texas Southwestern Medical Center, author of *Divorce Poison: Protecting the Parent-Child Bond from a Vindictive Ex*

The authors of *Shared Parenting* share both their professional and personal experiences and knowledge in the area of parenting and families. Their practical style of writing gives parents real situations to think about and the practical tools to find ways to really share the parenting and to continue meaningful relationships with their children after the breakup.

This is a must-read for any parent contemplating separation and divorce or for those already in the process. It's never too late to reconnect with your children. The short- and long-term benefits for parents and children far outweigh any immediate difficulties. You and your kids deserve this.

Judy Radich, National President, Early Childhood Australia

Research all over the world has shown that it is best for children to have both parents actively involved in their lives despite the parents' separation, except where there is child abuse, ongoing violence, or intractable conflict. This book is an excellent resource for people who want to understand how best to put the children first and to work out cooperative, shared parenting arrangements after separation. It is full of useful information, practical wisdom, and sensible advice. I recommend it very highly.

Patrick Parkinson, Professor of Law, University of Sydney

Negotiating parenting time following separation is complex and emotional, and often a source of ongoing conflict. This book offers practical solutions focused on children's needs, while challenging some traditional assumptions about parenting after separation.

Anne Hollonds, CEO, Relationships Australia (NSW)

Shared Parenting

Shared Parenting

RAISING YOUR CHILDREN COOPERATIVELY AFTER SEPARATION

Jill Burrett and Michael Green

Celestial Arts
Berkeley

Library of Congress Cataloging-in-Publication Data

Burrett, Jill F.
  Shared parenting : raising your children cooperatively after separation / Jill Burrett and
Michael Green. — 1st American ed.
      p.   cm.
  Originally published: Sydney, Australia : Finch Pub., 2009.
  Includes bibliographical references and index.
  Summary: "A guide for separated or divorced parents who want to develop a
cooperative, child-focused parenting approach, with advice about communicating
effectively, devising a shared parenting plan, establishing joint involvement, and more"
—Provided by publisher.
  ISBN-13: 978-1-58761-346-3 (pbk.)
  ISBN-10: 1-58761-346-8 (pbk.)
  1. Parenting, Part-time.   2. Children of divorced parents.   I. Green, Michael, 1939–
II. Title.

  HQ777.5.B87   2009
  649'.1—dc22   2009019727

Printed in the United States of America

Originally published in Australia by Finch Publishing Pty Ltd.

Design by BookMatters, Berkeley

10 9 8 7 6 5 4 3 2 1

First American Edition

Contents

9 27

122 241

Introduction

Shared parenting is the new way to look at parenting after separation and divorce. In many countries (including the United Kingdom, the United States, New Zealand, Canada, and Australia) cooperative shared parenting has for decades been rightly regarded as the best way of ensuring children of divorced parents adjust well to family change, so in many ways it's actually nothing new. But because for so long it's been presumed that dads either can't or don't want to be involved more often than one weekend every other week (and even that they aren't sufficiently competent to do more!), equal shared parenting seems new, challenging the assumption that upon separation children live with one parent or the other. For far too long there's been a misguided belief that children, especially those under ten, are better off with mothers—and this has helped to spawn another (hotly debated) belief: that the legal system disadvantages fathers.

We believe that this situation has seriously disadvantaged children, and that fathers should be more engaged with their children than they have been. This requires real time, just as most mothers have always known—and have given. We also believe that, for a very long time, gender stereotypes, "the system," and other complex prejudices have discouraged some fathers and caused others to participate little in parenting, especially after separating.

We don't think that one-weekend-every-other-week parenting is meaningful shared parenting. Shared parenting means being engaged with your children for a flexible 35 to 50 percent or more of their available time.

Studies on separated parenting are currently being conducted in many countries and focus particularly on whether there should be a presumption that equal shared parenting be the norm. Mostly, research has been unable to provide clear answers that would point to a general policy on this matter, since every family is different and some, sadly, are seriously dysfunctional. Families who use welfare services and courts, and cannot arrive at satisfactory solutions through mediation and counseling services, are very likely to be families where shared parenting isn't going to work for the children.

A general presumption of equal shared parenting therefore has some hazards and is unlikely to become official policy or law. However, its serious contemplation as a basic presumption is a good start toward de-marginalizing fathers, who need and deserve encouragement.

Fathers' protest groups (such as Fathers4Justice in the UK, Papà Separati in Italy, and SOS PAPA in Spain) have sometimes found themselves forced to take extreme measures in order to get attention in policy-making circles and have sometimes risked disrepute to get their views heard. For instance, one member of Fathers4Justice, dressed in a Batman suit, perched himself on a ledge of Buckingham Palace. Batman suits were also worn by several protesters outside the Colosseum in Rome. In Madrid, two men—protected by fireproof suits—doused themselves in gasoline and set fire to themselves outside the Spanish Parliament.

A radical overhaul of contemporary parenting policy and practice is long overdue. Exclusive maternal custody, with the mother doing all the parenting and the father merely paying the bills and pop-ping into the kids' lives from time to time, isn't really good enough for children—and often not for mothers—in either separated or "intact" family situations.

This is what we want to do:

- Help both of you be realistic about what's possible for your family, in your own unique circumstances. Gearing your life around children's real needs demands great self-sacrifice and compromise. If you aren't really up to full-on shared parenting, maybe you shouldn't be signing up for it. If you are, we want to encourage you to do it well.

- Help you to be responsible and creative about separated parenting. We recognize that for many mothers, shared parenting is difficult to contemplate, and for many fathers, it's difficult to achieve.

- Discourage you from following misguided advice from the wrong people and help you get reliably informed about the myths and realities of child psychology and legal precedents.

- Help you avoid using the legal system except for its mediation and information services.

About this book

We are aware of the various terms used throughout the United States and Canada to describe cooperative parenting after separation: co-parenting, time-share parenting, shared decision making, joint physical custody, and others. We've called this book *Shared Parenting* so that it's obvious we're talking about co-parenting with equal or close-to-equal amounts of time with your children. How-ever, we want to discourage parents from competing over percent-ages of hours, days, or nights. How much time the children spend with each of their parents must be about what's going to work well for them, not about what's fair for you.

We make many references to parent education and parenting programs, but detailed coverage of these is beyond the scope of this book. Many good courses and self-help books are available. (See Helpful Resources at the end of this book.) We confine our discussion of parenting after divorce to time-sharing specifically.

We have divided up our text into what seems to us logical sections, wanting to keep it easy to read. We base what we have to say on our own research and on our experience of what works and what doesn't for real people who have consulted us professionally over the years. We've also drawn on child development theory and the results of reliable research reports, mainly from Australia, the United Kingdom, and the United States. New research is happening all the time, stimulated in particular by increasing recognition among policy makers of the importance of active, engaged parenting. In order to encourage you to explore further the research we rely on, we have referenced this in the Authors' Notes at the end of the book.

We believe that research on patterns of parenting after separation has not so far been able to reliably demonstrate a preferred way of dividing parenting time for all families after separation. However, our research and experience shows that the best outcome for your kids is competent parenting that is genuinely child-focused, however you divide up the time slots, provided you both have plenty of time with them.

Jill Burrett and Michael Green

Personal reflections

Jill

I first had the idea of another book on separated parenting because in my consulting practice there seemed to be new kinds of issues presenting themselves for people facing separation. I recognize that many parents don't seek the advice and counsel of psychologists because they make their own private arrangements, so my clients aren't necessarily representative across the board. But because of the high profile that shared parenting has been getting lately, I am being approached by some parents who are very troubled at the prospect of sharing their children, as well as by parents who are keen to share the care of even very young children equally.

Although I have survived a divorce (albeit after a childless partnership) and have been a keen stepmother for twenty-four years as a consequence of my second marriage, I have not had the experience of shared parenting except through my clients. However, I do know personally about how your feelings can run riot when you're hurt and disappointed because your partner lets you down—distorting your judgment for a long time—and how a person you really loved and committed to can turn from a soul mate into someone from a different planet, impossible to see eye-to-eye with. I also know personally about a long-distance shared parenting arrangement that somehow survived the years of geographical separation because of goodwill, tolerance, acceptance, and a positive outlook. These attitudes are important—in fact essential—for shared parenting. And I do know firsthand about the very strong bonds that can develop between half siblings despite their different upbringings.

As a mother myself, as well as a child development expert, I am gravely concerned at the idea of a newborn baby spending seven days with one parent and seven days with another. My concern extends to the not-so-newborn, who—quite naturally—have to make the transition through the months from infancy to toddlerdom, and who will not thrive if their attachments to important caregivers are regularly interrupted for significant lengths of time (i.e., days at a stretch). I'm also concerned about parents being so protective of their children that they unwittingly discourage the development of emotional independence by limiting time with their other parent for the wrong reasons. However, I have always felt that fathers ought to be more involved with their children than they seem to feel they're expected to be, or than their ex-partners sometimes allow them to be. I believe that if parenting responsibilities were shared more equally in all families, children would not only be better off, but there would not be so many difficulties sharing children after a separation. Something radical needs to be done to encourage fathers to share effectively—and to help mothers share at all.

How is more equally shared parenting after separation going to work? How can it truly benefit children, given that it isn't what most parents have in mind when they commit to partnership and parenthood? And given that many parents seem to get caught up in notions of entitlement and fairness that don't have much to do with their children's emotional needs? A new look at separated parenting was obviously needed, and writing with an experienced father (my coauthor, Michael) was absolutely what was required! I wanted to challenge old assumptions and to help fathers and mothers enhance their parenting and look honestly at their motives and attitudes, so they have the best chance of getting it right. So I took another hard look at what was and wasn't working, and what the new research is showing—that is what has guided our advice and ideas as this book has come into being.

Michael

Why is it that so many separated men and women are unable to sort out sensible parenting arrangements without a massive amount of anger, bitterness, and trauma—to say nothing of the accompanying waste of time, money, and energy?

The key mistake made by many couples is not to accept that their world has changed. Separation and divorce changes the world for mothers, fathers, and children. It is not the same world any more. The family is a different family, the father is a different father, the mother is a different mother. The relationships between children and parents are irrevocably changed, no matter where or with whom they live. So everyone has to change too. For children, the experience is especially traumatic and painful and should not be underestimated. It is a betrayal of the trust that was given to them when they were born, a rupturing of the contract by which their parents promised that they would love and care for them together. It represents the loss of the world as they know it.

However, the good news is—and research confirms it—that children can survive the experience, and even thrive in their new family situation. And that's precisely what it is, a new family. If a separated couple can manage to see it that way, they are off to a good start. If they don't, there's a rocky road ahead.

It follows then, that if separation has to happen, it must be managed in a child-focused and sensitive manner. Right from the outset, when they announce that they are to live apart, parents should both take responsibility for what is to happen, tell the children honestly about arrangements, and above all, assure them that they will be loved and cared for by both parents.

Studies over the years have consistently shown that *the worst part of divorce for children is the loss of one parent*. Failure to acknowledge this can lead to a mother striving to establish a home situation that is unchanged in all aspects except one: the father is no longer there. Or it can lead to a father seeing himself in the same role as before: the provider who has limited, infrequent contact, and leaves it to the mother to do the nurturing. It results in the children having one home base, one close parental relationship, and one distant one. Not many separated parents are happy with this. Women, wanting to reestablish themselves in society and work, find the burden of parenting alone overwhelming. Men find that they have so little meaningful time with their children that they are reduced to onlookers in their lives. And all the research points to children being very unhappy with this outcome and wanting something quite different. What they want is a true relationship with both parents, and real time to foster it. This is what shared parenting is about.

What is shared parenting? It is an arrangement following separation whereby children have two homes and spend substantial amounts of time—including weekends and weekdays—with parents who share in their upbringing and development. In practice it means the following:

- Children spending ordinary and fun times with each parent
- Children sleeping, eating, working, and playing in each home
- Each parent listening and talking to the children
- The parents sharing the big decisions about the children's lives
- Each parent being involved in the children's schools, sports, music, and other activities
- Each parent being fully aware of the physical, intellectual, and emotional health of the children
- Children being part of two extended families—grandparents, uncles and aunts, cousins, friends

My views are based on over fifteen years' experience with separated couples: in the courts, in mediation, in group work, and in individual counseling, as well as on my own personal experience as a separated father. I have done a lot of reading and research in this area of human behavior. Opinions and conclusions differ and can be subjective and untested, but I think there are some common themes. In preparing material for this book, I spoke to many separated mothers and fathers who were practicing shared parenting. Their responses—some of which are included in the following pages—were remarkably similar. It was tough at first, but it worked because they did the following:

- Recognized that their world had changed
- Accepted that they—mother, father, and children—had to change
- Put to one side their anger, bitterness, and emotion
- Put their children's welfare before their own comfort
- Communicated, got help, and learned
- Acknowledged that their children wanted both parents
- Stuck at it

one

Parenting after separation

Separation always disrupts the familiar patterns of family life. Routines and responsibilities that have established themselves as the family grew and developed have to be renegotiated. How your family operated probably came about without a lot of proactive planning. It's unlikely that either of you parents worried too much, especially in happier times, about who did what and how much actual time you each spent doing the hands-on stuff of day-to-day family life, even though sometimes one of you might have felt unfairly overloaded or unsupported!

> It was the biggest emotional upheaval of my life. There are so many clichés about breakups being bad, damaging, and bitter, although ours wasn't. It was just the sheer sadness and disappointment that things didn't work out how we'd planned, which at times I found overwhelming, that was the hardest part to deal with while trying to be positive about the future for the kids. —*Naomi*

Why families work well

Even though today's breakup rates seem to seriously suggest that something about committed partnerships isn't working, traditional family life does work for children, if not always for parents. It has its own built-in efficiencies, which are useful, even if whatever might be happening between Mom and Dad isn't too good. Children can see both of the most important people in their lives (you two!) every day. Busy parents can feel in touch and connected with everyone on very little time. One parent covers the lion's share of the domestic minutiae of lunch boxes and spelling lists, and gets increasingly efficient at it. The other spends more time at work away from home (and becomes increasingly efficient at it), and spends more time with the family on weekends. Each parent takes on areas of responsibility that fit his or her skills, availability, and interests, and a natural division with commonsense delegation of domestic activities develops. Your adult partnership needs are met at home with your children's other parent. Whatever partnership frustrations and disappointments you are struggling with, the family you have created is the only one your children know and is what they depend on totally for their security. It's an effective and uncomplicated arrangement for your kids that meets their growing needs even if it doesn't always work for you.

Why separating means facing big changes

Because you're living separately in two different homes, everything changes. There's no overlapping. When you're on duty, you have to be able to meet all the kids' needs, and at the same time find a way to have a life for yourself outside of the parenting arena. You have to adjust to a system of parenting in shifts, in which you are completely on or off. You may have to go for days without seeing your kids, and you might not have bargained on making that adjustment until they were much older. You might have blended your working life during the week with brief family interactions in the mornings and evenings, with the really fun stuff on weekends and on family vacations. But separation puts an end to this. You might have expected your hands-on weekday routine to last for years to come, and your future was already set. Now the kids are off to their other home for parts of the week, leaving you feeling stranded and unsettled.

> At the beginning, I really missed my son when he went to his father's home. I felt cheated of my motherhood, restless, and unsettled when he wasn't around me. I cried a lot. But gradually it all fell into place. —*Jane*

Staying in a relationship that isn't working because you're dreading being an out-of-touch, occasional parent is about as unsatisfactory as staying in one because you're afraid of separating and having to share your children with their other parent for long periods of time. Both of these apprehensions are quite natural. By and large, moms still do most of the hands-on parenting and presume that they are going to continue this after separation. So they often resist shared parenting. On the other hand, dads who have assumed a breadwinning role may not have done much hands-on stuff and may be apprehensive about having an occasional parenting role after separating. However, given the opportunity, they may be prepared to make lifestyle changes to progress to fuller parenting responsibilities.

The scene is set for you both to start worrying about a minefield of potential grievances and uncertainties: what's fair, what's right, how to juggle everything so you don't lose touch, whether the kids will love you less if you're not there all the time, who's going to pay for everything to do with the kids, how a parent who's never been around much for them can look after them properly, and so on. Research on the outcomes for children of divorce has produced varied results. However, there is agreement that separation can put children at serious risk in a number of ways. Currently, about 80 percent of the children whose parents are separated live in sole-mother custody arrangements, and as many as a third of them have little or no contact with their fathers. The common arrangement for parenting children after divorce—living with Mom and visiting

Dad—often leaves everyone dissatisfied. There is evidence that it does little for solid parent–child relationships and can reduce one parent to onlooker status. Children cared for mainly by mothers can too easily lose contact with their fathers. Mothers can find parenting on their own a tough task and need relief and support. Fathers who experience difficulties maintaining contact often withdraw from their children's lives, with negative consequences for themselves and for the children.

But recent research brings us good news: children in shared-care arrangements are more satisfied and appear to be better adjusted on several levels; and many studies show that most parents with majority care want their ex-partners to see more of the children.

Your children will not suffer long-term effects from the separation if they have time with both of you—and if you both support this arrangement amicably and flexibly. They will suffer if you only think about what's fair for you, and if you criticize or interfere with each other's parenting.

> Shared parenting gives both parents the opportunity to
> be real parents. The kids develop a strong relationship
> with both of you. You don't have the burden that single
> parents have, and you avoid the desolation of being a
> "non-parent." —Jim

What should parents do?

As yet there is no scientific evidence to back a preferred way of dividing parenting time after separating. Because families are all so different, no one post-divorce arrangement can be said to be in the best interests of all children. What is certain, though, is that competent parenting is more likely to produce a good outcome for your kids, however you divide up the time slots. It's how you parent, not how many hours you put in, that matters, although quantity of time is relevant because it supports quality parenting.

We tend to approach parenting as if it's a talent that just comes because we became parents. But it takes insight, patience, self-sacrifice, and regular self-analysis, especially in today's challenging times. Separation is a great opportunity to rethink your parenting priorities. Your children need time with both of their parents, time that is meaningful. They need to feel you are available to them. They need you to give them guidance, sympathy, discipline, comfort, and supervision. They need for you to convey a strong sense of their importance to you despite your other priorities and interests. Quality parenting takes time, but having time with your children is no guarantee in itself that your parenting is going to be meaningful and constructive, unless you make sure it is. What your kids want, need, and deserve is emotional commitment and active participation from both of you, however their time with you is divided, provided you both have plenty of time with them.

Shared parenting can produce happier children and more satisfied parents

Shared parenting allows both parents substantial time with their children, during which they have full responsibility for day-to-day decisions about them. There is no "major caretaker" or "custodian" of the children, no "part-time" or "visited" parent. Time-sharing may be equal, or something approaching that. Both parents share responsibility and authority for their children's upbringing; both are acknowledged to be equally important for the emotional, intellectual, and physical lives of their children; both have the duty to foster their own and each other's healthy and meaningful relationships with their children.

Consider a radical overhaul

"Equal time-share," "fifty-fifty," "joint custody"—whatever you call it—may not be the best solution or the most practical, desirable, or

> Q: Is it realistic to have a child regularly spend weekends away from friends, belongings, and usual activities?
>
> A: Going out of their neighborhood every weekend or every other weekend can become unattractive for children as they grow older, when friends, sports, and social activities become more important to them. Some dads have their own weekend activities and expect their kids to fit in with them, almost as if they lived there all the time. All these factors can contribute to contact with Dad seeming like a meaningless duty, with children feeling unimportant to him and not really connected with his life. If weekends are really all you have, then make them as child-focused as you can.

affordable one for all sorts of reasons. But there's no reason why your starting point for planning how you organize yourselves shouldn't be a level playing field. Your children are your equally shared responsibility, after all. This was your starting point for family life as you planned and expected it to be, and separating shouldn't and doesn't need to change this. Try not to allow what's always been the pattern in the family limit what might be possible in going forward. In other words, keep an open mind. Whatever has happened between the two of you that caused you to separate, and however angry or resentful you might feel about it, your kids need you both, and preferably not with one of you having greater control of their lives and the other one being marginalized and "put out to pasture."

> If you have to divorce, this is the best possible way to look after your kids. Being involved in every aspect of the kids' lives—sickness, school, friends, birthdays, et cetera—is wonderful. And they like it that way. —Jack

So start thinking about parenthood continuing as fully as possible for both of you, however it seems to be divided on the calendar;

about the scope for engaged parenting developing in new ways; and about what changes (in attitude and output) you're going to have to make if shared parenting is to work well for your children. This book aims to help you do just this.

Successful shared parenting means the following:

- Putting your children's welfare ahead of your own feelings
- Believing that your children love and need two parents
- Recognizing and accepting that everyone is different, and different in their parenting
- Working out a parenting plan that is creative and flexible
- Keeping at it through thick and thin

It can work, and children today will benefit enormously if there's more of it. But it will be challenging.

A few guidelines for making it work

- You'll need maturity, easy-goingness, tolerance, commitment, confidence, a genuine child focus, and a sense of detachment about what happened to your relationship (so it isn't still preoccupying you).
- If you both have similar value systems and are from similar cultural and economic backgrounds, there will be fewer sources of difference and competitiveness between the households, and therefore fewer adjustments for the children to make at changeover.
- The two households need to be geographically close to each other. It requires a great deal of capital to maintain two homes suitable for ordinary life, but they don't need to be equally well appointed.
- Parents' new partners and their children need to be introduced sensitively and gradually.
- Infants' time away from important caregivers needs special consideration.

- Children need to be encouraged to be independent, both emotionally and practically. You can inspire their self-confidence by supporting their natural right to form independent relationships with those important to them and by letting them be responsible for practicalities they are capable of managing.
- Be creative, involved, and accommodating of your differences!

• • • • •

Jill says: I've talked with many couples who started off quite uncertain about a time-share arrangement, but got used to it after a few initial difficulties. It requires a lot of trust and a lot of letting go. One parent was pleased when his daughter discovered his neighbor's child had a similar arrangement and both kids were going to be next door to each other in the same week.

Michael says: It's amazing how widespread it is now. The child of a friend of mine told me that several of his classmates are doing well in shared parenting regimes. Interestingly, in almost all cases the parents themselves had designed the arrangements without any help or interference from the legal profession or courts.

• • • • •

KEY MESSAGES

- Separation disrupts the familiar family pattern and calls for a new one to be established.
- Separated parents must face big changes and be open to new ways of doing things.
- Shared parenting is usually the best post-separation arrangement for both parents and children.
- With shared parenting, both parents share the responsibility more or less equally.
- With a bit of effort, patience, and consistency, shared parenting will work.

two

Benefits and challenges

Every family is unique. At separation, each will have its own strengths and weaknesses and its own special issues, complex and challenging or relatively straightforward. Whether or not you have more than your fair share of special challenges, we encourage you to retain your responsibility for your family; to think and plan with your partner what separating is going to mean for your kids; to take advice from reliable sources; to use counselors and mediators if you get stuck; and to be open to the idea that you may learn a lot that's useful from reading parenting manuals and attending parenting courses. As we noted in Chapter 1, it doesn't necessarily come naturally—especially for dads, who've been on the sidelines for generations when it comes to childrearing.

> I stayed a long time in a difficult marriage worrying about how the children would cope with only seeing their dad at weekends, thinking this was the usual pattern when you separate. It took a while to get our heads around the possibilities of doing something different, but Dave was able to rethink his working hours so he could have some weekday involvement. —*Sascha*

Getting advice

Many parents think they're supposed to go straight to a lawyer to be told what to do when they're separating. It's natural to think you need to protect yourself, find out your rights, and start thinking of yourself as an individual who is unable to rely on partnership in the same way anymore. But you know your children, and you know their parents. So think about why you're asking a stranger how to look after your children. What you work out as a parenting plan (see Chapter 8) is likely to be what works best for them. Lawyers are useful if you have to get adversarial, but don't go there unless you really have to. Most specialist family lawyers do encourage self-responsible shared parenting and aren't always conflict enhancing. But remember, lawyers don't know your partner or your children, and they aren't trained in child or family psychology. In addition, they may be somewhat jaded by having to deal with really polarized, difficult clients, and so may be too ready to swing into adversarial strategies, unwittingly discouraging cooperative negotiations.

In many places—including the United States, Canada, northern Europe, Australia, and New Zealand—there are moves to go further than merely setting up mediation services to discourage litigation for family problem solving. Non-adversarial, multidisciplinary tribunals and easy-access information centers for parent education are now in place. Mediation, conflict resolution programs, and counseling have been shown to be successful in assisting separated parents to develop the attitudes and skills that enable them to become cooperative parents.

> We were doing okay—talking about the kids, even having dinner together, and I was spending a lot of time with the kids. Then we went to our lawyers, just to get some advice and see what we had to do about the divorce. Wow! Everything changed! I got a nasty letter from her lawyer, making all sorts of demands. I went around and asked her what was going on. She said her lawyer told her this was the

way it was done. She said she didn't know all the nasty stuff
would be in a letter.   —*Colin*

Doing it yourselves

Over half of separated parents have successfully sorted out their
own post-divorce arrangements with little or no assistance from
lawyers. How have they achieved this?

- By talking reasonably to one another
- By accepting that they are parents, not partners
- By getting as much information as possible
- By seeking help from mediators and counselors
- By learning to put their children's interests ahead of their own

Patterns of separated parenting are changing. Be creative and
open-minded about what's possible in your unique family. As you'll
know by now, we think that children need lots of real time with
both parents, and that for far too long fathers haven't been spending
enough time with their children, whether separated or not.

I downloaded a parenting agreement from the Internet,
mucked around with it, and gave it to my wife. She changed
it so much that we couldn't agree, so we took it off to a
mediator and he helped us knock it into shape. We'll have
to review it next year as the kids are young and things
change. But it's working okay for now.   —*Paul*

Let's now look at the main reasons why shared parenting can be
the best family arrangement after separation.

The benefits

There are many benefits to shared parenting, and it's reassuring to
know that they can outweigh the challenges that may pop up along
the way.

Sharing encourages cooperation

Cooperation between parents is an enormous plus for children, and shared parenting encourages cooperation because you can't share without cooperating. Neither parent feels left out of the family, and everyone is happier, especially the children. They can cope with their parents' separation, and even with their parents not liking one another very much. But children like to see their parents doing the decent thing and treating one another in a respectful and reasonable manner. They like to see them sorting out problems themselves within the family.

Sharing promotes amicable solutions

This is another important benefit of shared parenting: it keeps parents out of court. It promotes non-adversarial problem solving by requiring parents to talk to one another themselves (or with the help of a mediator) and to reach agreements that suit the whole family, rather than having a solution imposed by a judge. As discussed, involving lawyers and courts is expensive, time-consuming, and often traumatic. Children pick up the tension from their parents and find it sad and disturbing. They can cope with occasional blow-ups, but consistent and long-lasting conflict is seriously damaging to children.

Sharing fosters financial responsibility

There is reliable evidence that parents who have good relationships with their children pay more child support. Poverty is one of the more serious risks that children are exposed to after the separation of their parents. Lack of contact with an estranged parent is linked with lack of financial support. This, together with shouldering the major burden of raising the children, can make life difficult for the full-time parent. Shared parenting allows parents to feel that they are sharing the burdens and the pleasures of raising their children.

Q: I think he only wants shared arrangements so he can avoid paying child support. He's not really going to be there for the children, and my teenage daughter will end up doing lots of housekeeping for him. What should I do?

A: What does your daughter think about how a shared arrangement will work? If your fears are well founded, then your children may soon get bored. In this case you probably need to see a mediator to try to untangle the possible relationship between your ex-partner's parenting preference and financial considerations. Maybe your daughter will urge him to get some domestic help if she's feeling over-obliged to help. Maybe he'll do more than you think now that he's responsible for his own domestic space.

They both know what their children are doing, and they can see what they need for their education and development. They understand what it costs to provide a good upbringing for their children, and they are more inclined to be financially responsible.

Sharing ensures that neither parent is more or less important

With a shared parenting arrangement, there's no primary caregiver or custodial parent, as we explained in Chapter 1. Rather, the children live with and are cared for by both parents in turn, who start thinking and behaving as jointly and equally responsible for the children in different ways at different times. So we can abolish terms like "custody," "access," "parent visits," "residence," "contact," and so on. This helps children feel they are attached to both their parents, rather than to one "major" and another "lesser" parent.

Sharing helps separated fathers stay involved
so children don't lose out

There is a great range of attitudes among fathers. Some, whether they recognize and admit it or not, seem to have developed or grown up with the idea that fathering is an optional activity, and that close involvement with their children is something that they and their children can do without. Others see themselves as family- and child-minded, but don't actually do much parenting, being a presence but not an emotionally engaged one. Others again may see themselves as child-focused and be as engaged as they possibly can.

But regardless of Dad's approach to parenting, seeing his children only once every other weekend will make him feel outside the family, like a spectator on the sidelines. Even in families where Mom stayed at home to care for the children and Dad was highly involved in a job, Dad's position and influence were recognized, defined, and accepted by the whole family. After separation, however, occasional contact with Dad often has little meaning for children. It feels like compulsory visiting, nothing like family life. Fathers, feeling the shallowness and artificiality of the experience, lose confidence in their ability to parent, lose heart, and withdraw. And so they drift into estrangement. This isn't good for Dad's mental health and is even more problematic for his children. In contrast, shared arrangements give fathers hands-on time with their children, which means real closeness can develop, with obvious rewards.

> Sometimes I do get a bit bored over at Dad's, but I like seeing my cousins. My gran sometimes says things about Mom and I don't like this. She takes over a bit with the motherly things that Dad doesn't do, and that's really nice. —Kate, 11

All the research indicates that children hunger for the love and attention of their fathers and are deeply affected when they

Q: Do alternate weekends with Dad and Thursday nights for dinner provide sufficiently valuable parenting opportunities?

A: This traditional pattern—whereby the kids live with Mom and go to Dad only on weekends and perhaps one weeknight—has been accepted as the norm for so long, as if it's somehow of proven value. In fact, it can create problems for both parents: it can allow Dad to have all the fun, leaving Mom to deal with the hard stuff; and it can cause Dad to feel that this is all his ex-partner wants for him, and that it can't be enough. Instead, Dad could come up with a range of plans to discuss with her that give the children more time with him, and he could let her know that he really doesn't want to leave all the hard stuff to her. If either parent wants to insist on weekends only, the other shouldn't agree to it, suggesting instead a variant on a weekend, like Thursday afternoon till school on Monday, or after Saturday sports practice until Tuesday morning.

don't get it. They fail to understand what's happened, sometimes blame themselves for the situation, and are desperately sad. This can seriously damage a child's well-being, affecting not only their self-esteem, security, and scholastic achievement, but also possibly leading to feelings of loss and abandonment.

> I simply couldn't face the thought of going 12 days without seeing the kids and then only having them for two days, feeling like strangers. And knowing there was her new partner with them every day. It was easier to turn my back on it all and move on without them. —*Chris*

Important links with Dad's relatives can continue

If a father is discouraged from remaining or becoming involved, there are other consequences for mother, father, and children. A child may be cut off from the father's family—the grandparents, uncles, aunts, and cousins on the father's side. In addition, a decent and positive relationship with her ex-husband and his family can be of enormous support for a mother.

Fatherhood can become more involved and rewarding

Shared parenting presents a great opportunity for men to become better fathers. As we've said, for too long fathers have been the earners, expected to work long hours to support their families while the nurturing of children was left to mothers. The gradual development of family-friendly workplaces and the growing appreciation of father-involvement in the home and family is helping to change this. Fathers need to be willing to admit that if they haven't had a lot of hands-on experience with children, they're going to have to pick it up quickly. They should be open to the idea of consulting their ex-partners, their own mothers and sisters, attending parenting classes, reading books, and turning themselves into fathers with real capacity and expertise. This will be reassuring for mothers, wonderful for the children, and very rewarding for fathers.

Sharing can help mothers

By dividing the parental time commitment, shared parenting gives mothers more time off to further their education, to work hard to advance a career, or to simply enjoy some leisure time. Mothers with shared parenting may be less stressed and therefore better parents and workers: they have real time to look after themselves, knowing that their children are with someone important to them. Their other parent is in touch with the children and is a dependable pres-

Q: Is it right to consider a shared arrangement so that I can have childfree periods to devote my full attention to work? Will my children think I've abandoned them?

A: Shared parenting gives mothers better breaks and can enable them to get on with their careers, hobbies, and leisure activities more easily. Work is a reality of life that can be your personal creative outlet as well as a means of supporting the family. Shared parenting plans that are explained in consultation with the children will most likely be understood and accepted after an initial adjustment period. If you find they complain about the time you've agreed they have with their father—as if they're saying you've done the wrong thing—try not to feel guilty about this. Mothers are frequently torn by conflict between what they feel they are supposed to do, which is always put children first, and other parts of their lives they want to develop. Encourage your children to enjoy new ways of hanging out with Dad now that you're separated, and see how it goes. Remember, kids will often make irrational remarks to a trusted parent, so don't read too much into what they say, but keep a watchful eye on how things seem to be going.

ence in their lives, minimizing reliance on costly childcare. Both parents benefit by being involved in the children's lives and in decisions about them.

In a word . . .

Shared parenting exposes children to their whole world—the male and the female worlds of the two most important people in their lives. Lengthy periods, including days and nights, in both homes offer the children the rich experiences of different household routines, associations with different relatives and friends, and exposure to differing parenting styles. When children spend real time with two parents they have a sense of security in two places, not just one. The two households offer an expanded network of support.

The challenges

If we are realistic, we are dealing with a difficult situation, so any means of dealing with it—even the best possible solution—is going to have some built-in challenges that will have to be managed.

Sharing has challenges for mothers who can sometimes have trouble sharing

Mothers have to face major changes, too. They need to realize that despite their sense of guilt about leaving, or their outrage and hurt at being abandoned, or their deep disappointment in their partners, they have a responsibility to face what's happened head-on in the best way possible for their children. They must change their attitudes about themselves, their ex-partner, their children, and the relationships they have with them. Mothers tend to be the mediators of family relationships, including father–child relationships, in intact as well as in separated families. The great responsibilities of parenthood begin with the exclusive biological experience of mothers during pregnancy and childbirth. This sets up mothers to feel they are primarily responsible for their children. So they usually worry about the effects of their divorce on the children—perhaps more than dads typically do. They are anxious about the children's lives being radically disturbed or changed.

Later, this natural concern can sometimes take unhealthy forms. A mother may become so protective of the children that she limits their contact with their father in his new home and with his new partner. Or to compensate—in her own mind—for the separation, she might feel obliged to remain a full-time mother and stop or reduce work outside the home. Sometimes she sets unrealistic parenting standards for herself and the children's father. She may not trust the father to look after the children according to her standards. If one child is an infant and the father has not had the experience of much hands-on parenting, the mother will be worried about how the baby will fare. The primal nature of instinctive maternal care for the very young is difficult for some to understand and may be hard for some fathers to feel a part of. And maternal protectiveness may seem exaggerated if she is feeling hurt and abandoned by her partner leaving the marriage.

> It's easy to be nice for a week. You're so busy catching up and being loving, you never get to the real deep issues with your kids, the ones that make you close—except during holidays, in about the third week. I guess month-on/month-off might help this. . . . If you asked me about week-by-week sharing, I'd say—selfishly I guess—that I'd rather have them with me more of the time, just because I love them. —*Ruth*

A few words of warning

Shared parenting doesn't work for children when:

- There are very high levels of intractable conflict between the parents
- The parents are more focused on getting their fair share of time than on the real interests of their children
- It's a regime imposed because the parents couldn't come to an amicable arrangement, and they lack the goodwill to make it work
- A parent has plenty of time technically with the children but is not really there for them
- A parent's inattention causes children to feel unsettled or like visitors
- Children do not feel at home in both households
- There is inflexibility about the arrangements over time

We'll say more about parent versus child priorities in Chapter 6.

Sometimes shared parenting will be extra challenging

Many situations will test you. There will be times when you're irritated, exasperated, hurt, angry, busy, or merely inconvenienced. Managing these feelings may be beneficial for your children but will require a huge effort on your part, which has got to take its toll. Yet through it all you must also communicate and cooperate with your ex-partner as well as with your children.

Even if you've agreed to a shared arrangement, you may worry that your children feel you've abandoned them. You've always been a daily presence in their lives. This isn't an easy feeling to deal with.

> I had to get used to amusing myself a lot of the time when I was with Dad. He was often watching soccer. I used to wish I could go back to Mom's because she spent more time with me and I felt more important to her. —Joey

It's possible that you heartily disapprove of many things your ex-partner is doing with his or her life and resent having your children so affected by them. You may genuinely feel concerned that you're doing the wrong thing by the children in agreeing to a shared arrangement. Distinguishing between real and imagined anxieties when planning responsible parenting is a major challenge.

Perhaps you are in a situation in which you feel a duty to have more time with your kids than you can really find, and then feel bad that you haven't been more available for them when they are with you. Or, conversely, you really wanted to be with your kids so much that you took on more time with them than is turning out to be feasible, and you've ended up feeling you don't give them or your work the input that both these responsibilities demand of you.

Did you feel pressured to agree to a shared arrangement that turned out not to work for some reason, or wasn't ever going to be right for the kids? There may then be difficulties in changing the arrangements because it involves your ex-partner giving up some time with the children, and (s)he is not receptive to your views about the children's needs.

> We had an arrangement, which I was never really happy with, and I let myself be bullied into it. The kids seemed okay with it, but after a few years I felt they were really wanting more time with me. But I couldn't persuade their dad. He was quite sure they were happy with the arrangements, but I knew they couldn't tell him they weren't. —*Joanne*

You don't know what the future holds work- or relationship-wise. If one of you wants to move, it may mean that equal or close-to-equal shared parenting is no longer going to be feasible. Deciding which parent the children are going to spend more time with if there's to be a move may present difficulties. It's probably going to require a commitment to stay in the same neighborhood as your ex partner, or else reasonably close. Shared parenting requires sustained commitment, which you both need to think hard about before making.

If the financial settlement has yet to be decided, it could be causing you uncertainty, and you may be sensitive about the eventual outcome. It's going to cost more to have two homes adequately equipped for extended parenting periods.

Perhaps you don't want to have anything to do with your ex-partner. Maybe you feel that all this cooperative co-parenting just isn't for you. You may find that extended periods of parenting are frankly unrewarding and encroach on your freedom to explore new job opportunities, or to travel. It's possible that the on-again/off-again nature of shared parenting is difficult to adjust to, leaving you feeling unsettled and disjointed.

Once you've contemplated all we've outlined here in order to challenge any preconceived ideas you may have about separated parenting, take a long hard look at what's going to work for your children, for you and for your ex-partner. Take into account how your separation has affected both of you adults, your capacities, your ambitions, your attachments, your attitudes, and financial constraints. Consider the children's ages and temperaments. In short, examine honestly what you're willing to commit to in terms of being there for your kids.

Relationships for life

Through all the challenges, don't lose sight of two fundamental truths: First, children of separated parents do better if they have flexible, frequent, and meaningful time with both their parents (which is true in *all* families). Research shows that the children who adjust best are the ones who don't lose a relationship with a parent because of a separation. Second, the meaning in a parent–child relationship comes from what they do and say to one another when they are together. It largely comes not from the "fun" times but from what goes on when a parent comforts children after they fall, prepares food for them, reads bedtime stories, bathes them, and helps them dress. These everyday, very ordinary actions are the glue that bonds parent to child and child to parent. It takes time, availability, and repetition to make the bonding strong.

• • • • •

Michael says: Too many fathers leave it all to their ex-wife or ex-partner. It's up to fathers to learn the skills of real, hands-on parenting. They should also lobby for more family-friendly workplaces. With modern office systems and means of communication, it's not necessary for most men to be at their desks all day and half the night while mothers tend to the children's needs.

Jill says: You can't just gloss over the sense of loss that changing your family means. However much you know that your life will be better when separated, you're doing something that you didn't set out to have happen, and your children certainly don't want it. However much you're hurt by him/her having left, you've got to do what's best for the kids: try to imagine what it's like for them and do the right thing. Your ex-partner may not in your eyes deserve your open-mindedness and goodwill, having chosen this path, but your children need you to give them this.

* * * * *

KEY MESSAGES

- Get help if necessary: seek professional advice, check out courses/programs, read books (see the Helpful Resources section).
- If you and your ex-partner are on decent terms, you *can* do it yourselves.
- The benefits of shared parenting far outweigh any negatives: fathers stay involved and supportive, and mothers can get on with their lives.
- With shared parenting, both parents are equally important.
- Facing the challenges and dealing with change are essential to a successful shared parenting arrangement.
- Children of separated parents do better if they have flexible, frequent, and meaningful time with both parents.

· three ·

Popular myths

In this chapter we unravel some common myths about shared parenting and establish some realities. Sometimes separated or divorced parents are keen to work out a good shared parenting arrangement but are discouraged by the prejudices of friends or professionals. This chapter is intended to help those parents get past such objections.

> I sort of knew Mom and Dad were going to have to separate, and I worried about what this would mean down the track, having to see them separately. I was really hoping they'd just tell us how it was going to work out. It seemed to take forever for them to actually split and in the meantime they were just never with us together. —*Anthony, 10*

MYTH #1: Kids need to spend most of their time in one stable home

Reality: This is an understandable leftover from our hopes that our marriage would thrive and our kids would be in one happy home. It's also an unquestioned presumption put about by many lawyers and counselors. But it's a view that seriously underestimates the adaptability of children and fails to appreciate what is really important for them after the separation of their parents. The stability that children need is more than geographical stability. It is *emotional* stability, that is, the stability of meaningful, continuing relationships—especially the stability that comes from knowing that both parents love them and will be part of their lives, wherever they live. Constant conflict and competition between parents about how things should be done is obviously undesirable. Having one household as the primary home may seem to be an answer when there is persistent conflict between parents, but which one should it be? Should it necessarily be the one they're used to, to avoid more change? Or should it be the one where a real effort is made to foster the children's relationships with both parents and others who are important to them?

There's an even broader picture to consider. The emotional stability that's critically important for a child's healthy development comes not only from ongoing relationships with two loving parents, but also from the child's wider community. A child's sense of self derives in large part from knowing that s(he) has a place in the world—a real world made up of the community in which s(he) lives and grows. This includes the homes of both parents, and those of relatives and friends, the school, the movie theater, the mall, sports fields, and places where they meet friends, teachers, coaches, and others. And more importantly, the child's world is that bundle of relationships that arise from all those physical associations and the sense of belonging that all these important connections bring to the child.

We now live in a mobile society. This can create challenges for any child, but especially for a child in a separated family already burdened with the loss of united parents. You sometimes hear people use the stability argument against shared parenting; yet they are quite able to contemplate taking children out of their communities to different towns and schools away from relatives and friends. They may place children in childcare for long periods of time or send them to be looked after by grandparents, boyfriends, and babysitters. They may even enroll them in boarding schools. But they remain resistant to the supposedly unsettling idea of the children spending regular blocks of time with each of their parents, without questioning their own logic, or recognizing the inherent contradictions.

> We now have seven years' history of shared parenting. The children have never felt that they did not have two homes. They know they have two parents who love them. We are not jealous about them or our homes. —*Lionel*

MYTH #2: Kids need to know where they live and not be going back and forth

Reality: A clear, simple parenting plan plus goodwill and positive attitudes from both parents will quickly get children into a routine that will become part of their daily lives. Flexibility and compromise are always valuable, but to begin with it often works best to stick fairly closely to your original arrangements while everybody is getting used to being separated. Parents need to be on the ball, active and enthusiastic in their promotion of the plan. Hiccups need to be ironed out with a minimum of fuss. Regular reviews are a good idea, and not just when there's a problem. Breaking up a week or two into smaller chunks may mean that parents don't have to go so long without seeing their children, but it may also mean children are constantly on the go, always having to think of where they're supposed to be. Changeovers are often the hardest time, so when you're planning, lean toward a pattern that has the fewest changeovers, except for very small children. The challenges of going back and forth can be minimized by having two sets of everything (one in each home) and having regular days of the week associated with one home or the other. Having drop-offs to school and pick-ups after school can make the changeover easier for children.

Q: Surely my child will feel totally unsettled by the major differences in lifestyle and attitude we have. No sooner are they settled with me than they have to gear up to change over again. Is it better if the children stay in one place and the parents rotate?

A: This can work well, but it needs a dependable communication system to assist with smooth changeovers, and a high degree of dedication and positive spirit in both parents. If the idea is for them to stay in the family home where they have been living, this may only be possible for a time as the home may have to be sold for your financial settlement, at which point you'll probably both be getting a new place to live. Maybe you should initially consider two- or three-week blocks of time to allow for a proper settling-in before the children have to uproot themselves again.

MYTH #3: Infants under three should not spend nights away from their mothers

Reality: This view was based on outdated theory and is contrary to recent research. Attachment theory, first researched several decades ago, tended to emphasize the exclusivity of the maternal bond and its continuity as being crucial to healthy emotional development. It was argued that children from approximately eighteen months to three years old were likely to show unsettled behavior if separated from their primary caretaker for any length of time. This has led parents and advisers to conclude that a child under three should not be placed in overnight care of anyone other than the major caregiver, usually Mom. But many children nowadays have attachments to multiple people from a very early age and will be comfortable and settled with any of them, provided they are not separated from any one of them for an extended period. There is no consistent evidence that a night with their father is going to harm babies or toddlers, though individual circumstances are relevant. And if the children are well attached to the other caretaker (Dad), they should soon become used to him coming to them at night if needed, and doing everything else required. There is growing evidence that overnight stays in infancy form a meaningful basis for parent–child relations from an early age.

Sometimes it is Mom's needs and insecurities that make her reluctant to surrender her baby to the father for more than an hour or two. At times her own attachment to her child interferes with developing a suitable parenting arrangement. Maternal anxiety is a very powerful protector of young infants and therefore deserves respect (see also Chapter 2). Overnight contact with babies and infants (approximately up to eighteen months) is not in itself crucial for cementing parent–child bonds; daytime contact periods are the building blocks for introducing overnight contact later. Young babies are more settled (and their caregivers therefore less stressed!) if usual routines can be adhered to fairly closely, whoever is in charge.

MYTH #4: The more homey, hands-on parent is better equipped to do most of the childcare

Reality: Not necessarily, though this parent will have confidence and experience. The argument that this parent is more in touch with the children's needs and feelings assumes that it's only the quantity of time spent with a child that counts. Emotional bonds are created and strengthened by parents being available and doing things with and for children, but it's not just this. It's listening and talking empathically with your children, hanging out together, sharing parts of your life with them, helping them learn to discover independently, and so on, that creates bonds, not how many hours you spend on meals and school pick-ups.

Q: Surely it can't be right for our twelve-month-old to be away from me for long periods even though he knows his dad?

A: If he has had a fair bit of time with his dad during his life so far (with or without you being present), then he will have an attachment to his dad that means he's quite okay for increasingly long periods without you in Dad's care. Keep Dad informed about what routines you have established, not so as to make him feel he needs parenting lessons, but so he can respect your routines and have a settled baby to bring back to you, which will enhance your confidence in his care. An infant protesting about separations from one of you may need confident persistence, so he or she soon learns that leaving you does not interrupt that relationship permanently. See what periods are possible and extend them gradually. If Dad only wants a few hours several times a week at this stage, that's enough to sustain a growing attachment that can be built on later as your child gets older—even though you might want longer breaks now. Some dads aren't that good with babies on their own, so let his relatives help if they're local.

Children need time to do ordinary things with each parent, not just fun things on holidays and weekends. Just because your failing partnership and your work and/or other interests kept you away from home and hearth before you separated, that doesn't mean you're not important to your children. As we've seen, a silver lining to the disappointment of separating is that children get the chance to develop a closer relationship with parents who are committed to shared parenting but who weren't very available to their children before, and who can therefore develop their parenting skills more effectively. A parent who appeared to contribute little to family life deserves the chance to become a more involved parent, and children should not be deprived of the chance to forge a new, closer relationship with a parent if separation makes this possible.

Being open to this may naturally be hard for parents who have geared their lives around full-time parenting and who aren't confident that their ex-partners have the necessary experience to care for the children adequately.

> The lawyers would not entertain the idea—they ratcheted up the antagonism. I wanted to be a sole mother, and the court made orders for contact every second weekend. But my husband refused to accept being a weekend father. So eventually I gave in and we bought apartments near one another and started shared parenting. It's been for the best. —Jan

MYTH #5: It's not the quantity of time that counts, it's the quality

Reality: The cliché of "quality time" is sometimes used by judges, lawyers, mediators, and counselors to console fathers who spend limited time with their children. What you do with your time together certainly matters, as we pointed out in Chapter 2. Authoritative and engaged parenting creates emotional bonding between father and child, which contributes significantly to the child's well-being. These are two important elements of quality parenting. When children sense that their fathers have clear and fair rules for them that are mostly consistent (i.e., authoritative), they feel safe and secure. And when children feel close to their fathers (i.e., engaged with him), they feel better about themselves, do better at school, and have fewer behavioral problems. Exactly the same thing could be said of mothers, of course, who may technically spend hours with their children, but not actively engaged in parenting. If you are simply unable to spend any more time with your children than you do now, then there's even more reason to examine the quality of what you do when you are with them. A father in a shared parenting arrangement who is in fact often quite disengaged from his children, for whatever reason, is not going to build a meaningful emotional bond with them just because he is putting in the hours. But common sense and logic tell us that a close parenting relationship demands lots of time!

MYTH #6: Where there's conflict between parents, there should be little or no contact

Reality: People often seem to reach for the easy solution to conflict. For example, a mother finds that she and the children are upset after Dad drops them off. Perhaps there was a heated exchange over money or a late return. She jumps to the conclusion that the way to handle this is to limit their time with Dad. But the problem isn't directly related to their time with Dad; it's with the changeover itself. Money and punctuality are adult issues that affect the children because they are being involved in them when exchanges take place between parents in their presence.

Another possible situation is that the father finds that every time he sees his ex-partner she complains about the way he takes care of the children, and does this in front of them. He decides that the only thing to do is to reduce his time with the children. Again, it's the changeover that needs looking at, and it's lack of parental communication that is the problem. Minimizing the frequency of changeovers and/or not having direct contact with one another at drop-offs and pick-ups will safeguard the children's well-being.

Professionals—lawyers and counselors—sometimes suggest that the only solutions to ongoing conflict between separated parents are these: to reduce or eliminate contact between the parents themselves, to reduce or eliminate time between father and children, or to have supervised pick-ups and drop-offs. This conclusion is inconsistent with research, which shows that good contact arrangements result in reduced conflict between parents, and that there are better ways to manage conflict, for example, through counseling and educational programs. Limiting children's time with a parent to settle parental conflict is shortsighted and may set up loss of a relationship, which is known to cause serious problems for a child's development.

In the face of parental tensions, children tend to align themselves with one parent, seeming to imply that the other parent is the one at fault. However, this is a potentially misguided assumption as to what the child's behavior actually means: it confuses the picture for parents and their advisers, and so should not be the basis for any alteration of your arrangement. Rather than seeing hostility as a disincentive to shared parenting, it would be better to view it as an indicator that a better parenting plan is needed. Consideration should be given to agreeing on some rules, for example, no arguments in front of the children, no discussion at changeovers about adult issues (money, schooling, health, and the like), and basic courtesies at all times.

Sadly, there are some cases where, at least in the short term, more serious action is required. Where the incidence of conflict or violence is ongoing and major—such that it impacts significantly on the children—and remedial attempts are unsuccessful, that is the time to make real changes. Clearly this kind of situation calls for developing strategies to keep mother and father away from one another, and contact will have to be managed in a different manner. Parents should take steps to eliminate serious and repeated conflict, reminding themselves that it is clearly damaging to their children. They need to learn to manage their communication, if not in a friendly way, then at the very least in a business-like manner (see Chapter 10).

> In the early days there were lots of arguments. But we gradually got into a pattern and it all fell into place. Sometimes it's better to ignore problems and deal with them later—many problems are passing or are the result of looking too far ahead. —Marion

However, *conflict*, like *violence*, is a broad term. It can indicate anything from raised voices to serious violence—verbal, emotional, or physical. Not all parental conflict is harmful for children. There is a certain amount of conflict from time to time in all human relationships, and children can cope with this as well as adults. After separation, it's tempting for parents to place demands and expectations on behavior that are unrealistic and unreasonable. They are often sensitive and anxious about the children and therefore extra-ready to criticize or to worry too much about what the children say and do. They may subject themselves and their children to a level of scrutiny that they never applied when they were together and that is not applied in even the happiest of homes.

MYTH #7: Shared parenting works only when parents can collaborate

Reality: This is not necessarily true, although effective parental collaboration is always desirable. It's a pity if lawyers, judges, and counselors discourage shared parenting when collaboration is lacking, because it may discourage parents from trying to develop better collaboration or from embarking on shared parenting with a clearly mapped-out parenting plan that requires minimal collaboration. It also contributes to the myth that shared parenting is not desirable just because judges are often reluctant to make shared parenting orders. But this is simply because judges only make orders in highly contested cases, where parents are engaged in bitter, drawn-out disputes in which shared parenting is unlikely to work for the children.

Professionals sometimes assume that the problems they see in the cases they deal with are typical of the majority, but there is a whole world of parenting styles that they seldom examine because parents who have a successful plan in place don't need professional help. See Chapters 7 and 8 for more on collaborative and parallel parenting.

Q: Is it unrealistic to expect estranged parents to have the coordination and cooperation necessary for continuity? How important is continuity anyway?

A: We've argued that in terms of coordination and coop-eration you can't have too much of a good thing. Separat-ing may mean you're a bit short on this, at least to start with. But you can be coordinated and cooperative if you're really concerned about your children's welfare. Accept your differences and try to cultivate a kind of communication that recognizes them. For example, if you're worried about something that you don't think Dad will even be aware of, try some self-responsible communication like: "I know you'll think I'm a worrier, but could you please remember something for me so I can sleep at night? Sam really has to stick to that diet regime for another week before we see the specialist again—and do you mind if I email you again tomorrow with a reminder?"

In this way, you accept that you have a conscientious approach to what you're trying to do, and you ask him to help you rather than suggesting he's slack and/or disrespectful about your priori-ties. Children can quite readily adapt to interruptions to continuity between households, so differences should not in themselves dis-courage sharing. However, if collaboration is in short supply, please refer to what we say about parallel parenting in Chapter 8.

· · · · ·

Michael says: It's important that parents challenge the con-ventional wisdom because so much of it is based on precedent, folklore, unfounded assumptions, and prejudices. And there's such a variety of advice being given, it sometimes seems as if we're not supposed to know how to use our own creativity and common sense! Parents need to recognize that while it might seem easier and safer to follow established rules, the best solution may come from ignoring the advice and following their own instincts.

Jill says: I really applaud people seeking good advice and becoming as well informed as possible before making important decisions, even though parents really know their own children and their own circumstances best. Sometimes parents have to accept that there is no exact or perfect answer, that family life often falls short of ideals, and that we're all just trying to do our best in challenging circumstances.

• • • • •

KEY MESSAGES

- Myths need challenging and realities need facing.
- Children need two homes when they have two separated parents.
- Organize the program to suit your circumstances, not vice versa.
- Infants require special consideration when part of a shared parenting arrangement.
- Shared parenting allows both parents to be hands on.
- Both quality and quantity are important in parenting.

four

Some ifs and buts

Having explored some of the common myths, let's now consider some more topics that often come up and that are important to think about before you get into your real planning. They are designed to challenge your thinking constructively, to help you recognize your areas of misinformation, and to question your attitudes and possible biases.

Children's wishes

> I was very sad when Mom told me Dad was moving out. I didn't understand why he had to and I felt he was walking out on us. But I see him pretty often and we still do the same things together, although I often wish Mom was there too. —Adam, 6

Children can't possibly know what arrangements are going to be best for them, even if they might seem to know what they want. Children should have their views taken into account so that they feel listened to and taken seriously, but not so that they feel major decisions are being made by them, or left to them. When it's about how much time they spend with one parent and the other, asking them to express a preference is asking them to choose between their two parents. This is a dreadful position to put children in, unless both parents are very friendly and you can all discuss it together. If you can do this, congratulations. Children who seem to be saying they want equal time with their parents are usually saying they want to be fair, even if it doesn't really suit them. Don't mistake this expression for a rational, thought-out judgment.

So care needs to be taken in involving children in separation planning. Younger children are probably best told what arrangements you parents have worked out for them when you tell them about separating. Listen to their comments (including any protests and upsets) and confirm that you have thought it through with their best interests at heart and that you're going to see how it works for a while to see how everyone fares. Speaking authoritatively will reassure them that their parents are still working as a team, are in charge, and can tell everyone what's expected of them. Older children will want to have more say in arrangements as they grow into taking charge of their own lives in all sorts of ways. (See Chapter 6 for more on children's wishes.)

> We've had an evenly shared plan for three years now—
> they accept it. They don't like moving from one house to
> another, but they know that's the way it has to be if they
> are to have two parents. They didn't like their world being
> disrupted, nor having less money. —Anne

Parental differences

Children will adapt to quite different regimes if you reinforce each other's differences as parents and allow a settling-in period at the beginning of their blocks of time. Your differences as parents are not reason enough in themselves for not wanting a shared arrangement. A mother and father with different parenting styles can complement one another effectively. As long as you have an efficient system

Q: Does having two parents involved in everything just highlight for the child their differences?

A: It can if either of you is making a big deal of the differences. Parents are different, whether they are together in a family or not, and each has different things to offer children in the way that they each approach life. Highlighting differences isn't necessarily bad: children learn to deal with and respect them. It is criticism by one parent of the other that's difficult for them to handle. An example of non-competitive handling of differences would be to say to your child, "If Dad was deciding this, he'd do it this way, but my take on it is this. . . ." This conveys a certainty and a familiar acceptance of your differences as parents.

for informing one another (see Chapter 10) of relevant events and how you handled them, it won't matter if you deal with things very differently.

For example, if you allowed them to stay up late the night before they go to their mom's, and you know she's stricter than you are about late nights, let her know in a considerate way that they were up late, acknowledging your differences on this point. This can help a lot with the exasperation she might otherwise feel about having to manage cranky and unsettled children because you have shown some consideration of the possible effects on her of your different policies about late nights; and it will help prevent the children feeling Mom's tension over something you've let them do. Your kids are half you, half him/her and have a right to experience and make sense of your differences without undue tensions between you about them. Children living with both their parents together have to do this too, remember. You don't have to pretend to agree with what goes on in the other household, you can just say how you want to do things in your home. And don't go into too much explanation about why, or you will invite challenge and debate in response.

> Sometimes they'll tell me about what Dad does or doesn't allow. I say, "I'll check this out with Dad" or "That's his way, not mine." The new wife introduced new discipline—I talked it through with them. We negotiated it. —*Karen*

Letting them go

Getting used to having significant periods without your children is a difficult adjustment for involved and attentive parents. You may think they might want to tell you something or that they might think you've forgotten them. You might feel the need to say good-night or to be available for them just in case. You need to be really honest about who you are keeping in touch for. There's a fine line between keeping lightheartedly in touch and over-intruding. If you are really sharing parenting genuinely, then you don't need to check if they're all right—doing this conveys uncertainty to your children. And you don't need to be informed about where they are or what they're doing every moment of their time away from you. They don't need to be worrying about whether you're all right without them either. If something exciting happens, of course they'll want to call and tell you their news. You may miss saying goodnight every night because you always used to, but they'll be fine without your call.

Parents often think that no news or overlap between homes is because children are being prevented from communicating. But it may just be because they're fine, or because they quite unconsciously manage their two homes with useful boundaries between them. With longer periods away from your children, like holidays, make some arrangement about occasional contact that conveys trust and lighthearted interest, not self-interested surveillance! More on this in Chapter 10.

When to go to court

Many parents have very profound feelings about their situations, which definitely need a helpful outlet, but no one needs a day in court. Try to be honest with yourself about motives that are not completely child-focused but that have more to do with punishment, entitlement, vengeance, and so on. Think long and hard about what outcomes the court could come up with and whether any of them would in fact help the children or just create another set of ongoing issues. Only if you have exhausted all possible avenues for a self-determined solution or there are very serious child welfare issues at stake that leave you no option, should you go to court. Court-imposed decisions should be a last resort in very extreme cases. Going to court is unpleasant and traumatic, as well as emotionally and financially draining. Cases can drag on for months or years. Litigation exacerbates conflict between parents and increases pressure on children (see also Chapter 2). Children pick up on continuing parental conflict, and it can have seriously damaging consequences for them. It isn't good for children to know about lawyers, affidavits, oaths, lies, parents trying to outwit and discredit one another, nor to know that their loyalty to each parent is being assessed. This isn't what family life was meant to be about. Self-negotiated decisions in families work better and last longer than externally adjudicated ones, and there are many other ways—all less stressful and less expensive—to settle disputes.

Equal influence/Equal time

Even if you see your children much less than they see their other parent, you can still be close if you're practicing meaningful, engaged parenting. If you can have more time, it'll be even better for them. But time-sharing shouldn't be a competition. What do we

Q: Does more traditional separated parenting, with its clearer demarcation of responsibilities, reduce interparental competition?

A: It's not the plan that produces the conflict. Indeed, a good plan can protect the children from damaging parental competition. We think the clearer demarcation of responsibilities may be a default preference for some dads because they don't want to upset their ex-partners by taking too many established responsibilities from them. In a more traditional arrangement, dads can still give a lot of support by keeping in touch with what's going on; but if he can find more time to be actively involved, then both parents can find a way to be noncompetitive about parenting. Some counseling and parenting programs can be of great assistance here.

really mean by a *balanced* upbringing? If it's a case of both parents needing to have the same number of hours with the children to have an equal amount of input, it's likely that you're being over-focused on fairness, as if you feel uncertain of the strength of your parental input. Perhaps you're competing with the other parent for maximum influence or you're so critical or concerned about his or her input that you want to moderate it by maximizing your own. These are not usually truly child-focused reasons for wanting equal time. If you are concerned about your ex-partner's influence on the children, then this will be an issue regardless of your arrangement. And there's no guarantee that having equal time will affect how much influence you or the other parent has on the children. The way to be a real part of your children's development is to give them plenty of time and to do interesting things with them.

Creativity and open-mindedness

Parents worry about minimizing the disruption to their children that their separation is going to cause, but this shouldn't lead them to assume that Dad should go live somewhere else and Mom should simply carry on as she has been doing. In intact families, although fathers may spend more time at work than at home, they are still very much a part of their children's lives—and on a daily basis. They are with them every day and every weekend in the ongoing interactions of family life. This valuable connection that exists while he's part of the family can't happen in the separated family. The whole character of the family changes, and maintaining both parents' engagement with family in the new circumstances needs a creative approach.

Divorce can be a trigger for improved relationships between children and parents, especially between children and their fathers. Just because Dad didn't do much hands-on stuff with the kids before doesn't mean he can't start to do more. He'll want to do this to keep in touch, and he'll be fine if Mom encourages him and gets over her frustration that he didn't do more before the separation. Just because he now lives somewhere else doesn't mean he can't come around to pick up the kids and drop them at school, for example. Children can adapt to changes readily if these changes are explained to them with confidence and optimism.

Ideas for keeping both parents in touch with the kids

- Attend weekend sports events whether or not it's your scheduled time. Keep a respectful distance from your co-parent if that makes everyone more comfortable.
- Take off work early once a week to see the kids, hang out for a couple of hours, then drop them off.
- Get involved as a volunteer with something they do every week, whether it's your week or not.

- Encourage your children to be independent, helping them learn how to get what they need from whichever parent they're with.
- Negotiate ways that you parents can help each other with transport, meetings, and so on.

Kids adjust—they are flexible. They can deal with and conform to different rules in different households. They're cunning at times—they'll try to play you off against each other and manipulate you. But we don't make a big deal of this, and often it just goes away. There are no more arguments about parenting than when we were together. —*Brendan*

Rights and responsibilities

On most issues, where there is a conflict, parents must put their children's interests before their own. Children have rights and parents have responsibilities. Parents have these responsibilities once they have brought children into the world, and it is a child's right to have responsible parents. But parents have rights, too. Each parent has the right to a happy and peaceful life as an independent person, consistent with family responsibilities. However, parents should not be overly dependent on their roles as parents or defined solely by their worth as a parent. Moreover, all good parents have the right to participate in the lives of their children. A parent has the right—through time, activity, influence, and association—to provide his or her child with the opportunity to grow, learn, and develop as a person. Sure, this right can be lost if a parent is violent, physically or emotionally abusive, neglectful, or immoral. But in ordinary circumstances and in the great majority of families, parents are valuable to their children, and they have a right to be with them and to enjoy them. But just being a parent does not automatically guarantee you time with children ahead of other child-centered

Q: If one parent has to work full-time and the other works from home or doesn't work, how do you deal with the after-school care arrangements?

A: Depending on how you view after-school care (either as fun or as a very poor substitute for home life) and how many helpful friends, relatives, and neighbors you have, it may be best if the majority of the full-time working parent's time with the kids is on weekends, even though weekend time isn't representative of real life. See what can be done to negotiate leaving work early even if it's only a couple of days a week—some employers are becoming more flexible. Often some dovetailing between the parents will work. For instance, if you're doing week on/week off, it could be good if the kids see their less-limited-by-work parent midweek, so you can work late that day, then get a neighbor to have the kids another day, and leave work early once or twice a week, then you're nearly done without fobbing off the children too often during your busy week. Work is crucial, and children know and respect this.

considerations such as their emotional needs. You are not entitled by virtue of mere biology to have the care of your children for a given portion of time unless it is in their best interests.

Paid care or parent care?

Is it better for the kids to be looked after by their moms and dads (or other close relatives) than by anyone else? If they need child-care during their period with one parent and the other parent is available, should the available parent step in and take over? This is quite often a thorny issue. Let's imagine a dad who has become self-employed and can (at last) have flexible working hours and a mom who has a part-time job. Dad wants a week-on/week-off schedule but will need to have the kids in after-school care two days a week, which happen to be days when Mom isn't working and could pick them up after school. Mom is keen not to farm out the children too much, especially if a parent is available. Dad, for his part, thinks the kids quite like after-school care—and anyway, sometimes his mother will help instead.

It's likely that these two parents have quite different ideas about their children's progress toward independence. They may have different ideas about shared parenting. While it's true that parent–child contact is especially precious in busy, working families, it does often work better if Dad does things the way he thinks works best during his time, and Mom does things the way she likes to in her time, keeping what actually happens in each family respectfully separate. If Mom and Dad are getting on well, it may work okay if Mom does the after-school pick up in Dad's week, but going home to Mom's place may affect the kids' continuity with Dad. Dad's working hours are a reality of his life, and after-school care is often fun, or may be substituted for time with a relative on his side of the family. There are no clear rights or wrongs here; whatever the parents can agree on will probably be okay—and can always be tried and reviewed.

· · · · ·

Jill says: It's very important, when you feel exasperated about your ex-partner's parenting priorities, to take a step back and ask yourself: how much does what you're worrying about really matter, and what will be the real consequences of it for the children anyway? Worrying excessively about things you can't change is very debilitating.

Michael says: Seriously rethinking the difference between rights, responsibilities, and entitlement when it comes to parenting is a worthwhile exercise. You can apply your thinking to the ifs and buts we've presented here. Be careful, for instance, not to allow your outrage at the breakdown of your relationship to make your thinking become unhelpfully rigid and possessive.

· · · · ·

KEY MESSAGES

- It's vital to listen to children after separation and divorce.
- Different parenting styles are okay.
- Getting used to living without the children can be difficult at first, but you have to let them go.
- Stay away from court if at all possible.
- Noncompetitive parenting is the best way forward.
- Be creative and open-minded in your approach.

five

Sorting out your motives

The single most crucial factor for successful shared parenting is whether the two of you are genuinely approaching your parenting responsibilities from the children's position. Are you really being honest with yourselves about who shared parenting is for? As we noted in Chapter 2, recent research into shared parenting suggests that it works for kids if it's managed in a child-focused way but not if it's managed in a competitive, adult-focused way. This is an extension, in a sense, of the established principle that parental separation is not in itself automatically damaging to kids, but that bad parenting definitely is; and that parents often get entangled with their own feelings about the breakup at the expense of good parenting.

But what do we really mean by *parenting in a child-focused way*? And how do we know when we've got this wrong? Let's look at some of the attitudes and expressions that reflect a less-than-child-focused approach to separated parenting, and then you can take a really honest look at yourself with a list of questions designed to alert you to when you're in danger of not staying on track.

How your own feelings can interfere

I know Dad's really sad about what's happened. When he cries, I feel sad too and I wish I could fix it for him, so I give him a lot of hugs. But Mom is a lot happier and that's good. —*Claire, 7*

Children are happiest when their needs rather than the needs of their parents take priority. If children sense that their parents want to divide the time equally because each one can't bear the thought of the other one having more, the children feel more like possessions to be fought over than people to be loved. It is therefore obvious that it's the relationship between the parents that is the key to the children's happiness. When parents are in competition with one another about the validity of their grievances, it's difficult for them to distinguish between their own and their children's needs; they become inappropriately protective and/or controlling, and transmit their feelings about their ex-partner directly to the child. Many parents face separation with a sense of injustice and outrage at what's happened and with anxieties about the future. These sorts of powerful emotions affect your attitudes and behavior quite profoundly, often without you realizing it. Under the guise of wanting what you genuinely believe is in your children's best interests, you are expressing your own anxieties and insecurities through anger and vindictiveness. When you are destabilized by a partner leaving, you often protest by demanding fairness. ("You left the family, it's not fair to take the children too!") You unwittingly assume your children feel the way you do—abandoned. Your partner is leaving you, not the children, and (s)he needs your help to show them they aren't themselves being rejected.

Some parents have fears (usually unrecognized) of becoming less important to their children and see spending equal time as the only way to retain their place in their children's lives. Parents behaving as rivals for their children's affections is in fact a disguised form of competitiveness.

> For years I couldn't talk with my wife about her wanting to separate because I was just terrified of the prospect of losing touch with the children. It was as if it was an absolute certainty that this would happen when we split. Eighteen months after we separated, I realized I had developed a much better relationship with them than I'd ever had before. —*Anthony*

Sometimes child support obligations are a factor, though it's offensive to most of us to admit financial considerations are directing us. But you may not like the way your money is being used by your ex-partner, and if equal time means no money needs to flow to him or her, you'll be happier. You may also be afraid, or may hope, that whoever has more time with the children will somehow be entitled to continue to occupy the family home.

Some lawyers advise separating clients not to leave the matrimonial home until they have obtained agreement or court orders on all issues in dispute. This may be a useful tactic but it can place enormous strain on both parents and children. Parents with their children's welfare at heart will find a better way to sort out living arrangements.

You may have deep-seated, unacknowledged anxieties about separating from your children that are really more about your own fear of loss, of feeling peripheral; about fearing that your children think you're secondary to their other parent, and not needing you; about wanting to have as much influence on your children as their other parent, so as to feel confident about them; and about wanting to prevent your children feeling you've left them. You might doubt your own position as a valued or proper parent unless you have equal time. You may feel guilty that you've not been very involved as a parent until now, so you're afraid that you won't be missed and that the other parent will be preferred. These feelings are normal as you journey through your own emotional adjustment to separating, but they are largely about your own lack of confidence in yourself. They may have links to deep-seated aspects of your personality that are connected to, but far precede, your adult relationships. Recognizing these feelings for what they are and how they affect you now, perhaps through personal counseling, will improve your own emotional well-being. This will also help your children thrive: instead of worrying too much about you, they can get on with their own childhood—as they should.

> Shared parenting is a means to an end. It's important for the boys to know both parents, and I didn't want to be the wicked mom/witch, seen as depriving them of time with him. But I realize how powerless I am to have any influence when they are with their father. Mothers have to get past that and let go. —Brenda

You may want to retain your children out of vengeance, pretending that it's for their own well-being. (What sort of influence is (s)he on the kids, having had an affair?) You may want to punish your partner for withdrawing affection from you by insisting the children must be with you most of the time even when your other commitments don't make this very practical. Or you may be unable to contemplate letting the children have substantial time away from you because you feel doing so somehow supports the behavior of your ex-partner that you so disapprove of.

Why these adult feelings matter

> My wife had an affair, which I'm sure started before we separated. I was hurt, of course, but my big issue was, and still is, that doing this was a selfish and irresponsible way to deal with being unhappy with me and an appalling example to our girls, who have had to get used to the idea that their mother destroyed the family. —Mike

All of these are frequent motives for parents feeling anxious about equal involvement, and, while many of them are understandable, they are really about the parents' needs and feelings, not the children's. We're not saying you shouldn't feel these things, just that you need to know how they affect your attitudes, your thinking, and your abilities to compromise and be flexible. Most importantly of all, these powerful feelings can cloud your perception of your children's real needs, preventing you from being child-focused. If not addressed, they are likely to interfere with successful shared parenting arrangements. In other words, we're back at our starting point: it's not how the time is divided, or in what percentage, ratio, or proportion—it's how cooperative and mutually supportive the relationship is with your ex-partner that determines whether your arrangements will work successfully for your children. Children need to feel settled and at home in both households. They should not have to be constantly on guard about their behavior in one home for fear that it might upset the other parent.

> Separated parents have to get past hating, and focus on the children. They must avoid buying them off, getting in with them through regular treats. You've got to think of the children, not yourselves. —*Elaine*

Checking out your feelings

Seriously consider whether you feel any resonance with the following statements and the feelings that may be behind them:

"I'm angry that (s)he left me, and that (s)he's already got someone new."

"(S)he doesn't deserve to be with the children after what (s)he's done."

"I must counter his/her influence on the children."

"I must make sure the children like us equally. That's what's fair to them . . ."

"I don't like the idea of another man/woman seeing my children more often than I do—they've been through enough already without having to get used to another person as well."

"I don't like the way his/her partner raises his/her children and I don't want mine influenced that way. They're unruly and disrespectful."

"It is my duty to be there for my children at least half of the time . . ."

"It's not fair for the children unless they see me half of the time . . ."

"I can't have a proper influence on the children unless . . ."

"(S)he left me and wants to take the children away from me as well; (s)he broke up the family."

"Why shouldn't I drop by and see the kids even if it's not my week?"

"The kids will be totally confused if they don't have one place they call home."

"I have a right to see my children, they're half mine so I'm entitled to."

"I have to pay for their upkeep, so I should have a say in how much I see them."

"I hate asking for permission to see my children, so fifty-fifty would help me feel I have my fair say over things, that (s)he's not in charge of where they are, rationing my children out to me . . ."

"She won't ever let the children see me in her time, even though they say they want to sometimes . . ."

"(S)he keeps on setting up things so they want to see him/her for something or other in my week."

"I refuse to be just a weekend parent! I'll miss them dreadfully during the week and I can't give up all my own weekend stuff!"

"I know (s)he doesn't really want shared parenting, (s)he just wants to be difficult!"

Q: He's left and wants to involve his girlfriend with our children already. Surely they've been through enough without having to spend time with the person who caused our breakup being a mother to them?

A: It's always a good idea to slow the pace of family changes so as to respect everyone's feelings. You can ask him to delay her involvement because there isn't any hurry. Their time with Dad is supposed to be just that. But he's likely to think it's because *you* have a problem, not his children. One of the great challenges of separated parenting is one parent having a valid view about something to do with the children's feelings, which is dismissed as self-centered by the other. If he hasn't thought of the wisdom of putting off her introduction for a while of his own accord, he's unlikely to listen to you. In addition, your children will find it harder to adapt if they're made to feel that getting to know her upsets you. You don't have to pretend that you approve of what's being asked of your children, but you don't need to volunteer your disapproval. You can't really do anything about the situation, except support your children, who won't want to get to know her any faster than at their own comfortable pace. Encourage them to make the best of it, and to make sure they have plenty of time with Dad by demanding this of him. Most stepmoms, whether they are mothers themselves or not, are likely to respect your significant position in the children's lives and the importance of their relationship with their dad; and your children will make sure she doesn't take over. Remember, your duty is to raise children who respect and get on with people. You are not setting a good example if you demonize your ex's girlfriend to suit your own needs. You need an outlet other than your children for expressing your very real outrage at how things have turned out.

Behind all these expressions are motives such as lack of confidence, vengeance, retribution, outrage, lack of control, need to control, a sense of entitlement, self-centeredness, anger, anxiety, rivalry, and so on. They reflect adult-centered priorities. If you think you identify with any of them, spend some time questioning and reflecting on how valid they really are for you; and if you have a trusted friend, run your thoughts past him or her.

> When I hear Mom or Dad talking about their time with me, I feel they're competing, like I'm some kind of possession. I don't really think of my connection with them being measured by hours or days. They're different people and we do different things together which take different amounts of time. —*Amy, 16*

> I'd like to spend more time with Dad, but I know my mom would be hurt if I said so. Dad gives me a bit more freedom and we do action things together. I think Mom might be a bit jealous, and a bit lonely when I'm not with her. —*Jamie, 12*

> Mom tends to quiz me about my time with Dad as if she's worried about Dad not being a good enough parent. Sometimes if I tell her about what time I went to bed or what movie I saw, she gets really cross, and I feel I shouldn't have said anything. —*Sammy, 14*

Now we're going to ask you to do a self-check. Think carefully and be as honest as you can. There are no right answers. The questions are designed to help you decide what's going to work for you and your children. It won't hurt for you to do both the mom's and the dad's lists, as there's quite a lot of overlap.

Checklist for moms

1. Are you overly worried about the children being bored or neglected with their father? Might he not have hidden talents?

2. Are you perhaps assuming they experience their father the same way you experienced him?

3. Are you anxious about them resenting you for sending them to Dad's for more time than you think they want or need? That encouraging them to feel they have another home away from you is somehow rejecting them?

4. Are you anxious about missing them too much, as they've been such a full part of your daily life for so long?

5. Are you judging his parenting capacity by how he behaved as a father in the marriage? Can you entertain the idea that this may have been associated with your relationship and how you were both managing it, and that it doesn't necessarily reflect a lack of parenting skill or, at least, parenting potential?

6. Are you anxious about letting go of your children, afraid they might have too much fun or maybe even not want to come back to you? If he has family, a girlfriend, maybe other children, and you're on your own, might you feel uneasy about them comparing happy family time there with how it is for them in your home?

7. Are you ready to stand up for your way of parenting, without knocking his?

8. Are you ready to receive dirty clothes, torn uniforms, and bad-tempered, unsettled, exuberant children, without showing your frustration to them?

9. Are you afraid of not being important to your children if you don't have a majority of their time?

10. Have you got the skills and application to be all things (to your children) some of the time, as distinct from being some things to them all of the time—the disciplinarian and authority figure, as well as the warm and fuzzy talking/feeling caregiver?

11. Can you confidently bring to his attention something about the children in a style that's helpful, not directive?

12. Are you able to give your children the freedom to negotiate their own individual relationships with their dad, independent of your doubts, fears, and naturally protective instincts?

13. When they make comments about what goes on at Dad's place, are you able to lightheartedly listen, and not engage with them over what you think about it?

14. Do you think you're going to be able to deal with major differences in parenting practices in a way that supports both your and his way of doing things—even if you heartily disapprove of his—without engaging the children in comparisons?

15. Are you worried about the financial consequences (i.e., payment of child support) of him having more than a certain amount of time with them?

16. Will your confidence as a parent be undermined if you have less than equal time?

17. How would you feel if your children said they wanted to see Dad less? Or more?

Checklist for dads

1. Are you really going to be able to get off work early, however much you may want to? Are you perhaps taking on too much? Might the kids end up on their own more than you intended, with your eldest doing too much supervising?

2. Are you able to consider a request to go to Mom's during your time with an open mind?

3. Are you really up for dealing with the emotional demands and self-centered immediacy of children, especially tired and cranky ones?

4. Are you really aware of how much household work was accomplished when you were a family together that you took for granted—such as bedtimes, healthy eating, music practice, laundry, and math homework? Can you take this on? Or will your children feel the chaos of domestic disorganization?

5. Can you receive information about the kids from their mom without automatically feeling she's telling you how to parent?

6. When they make comments about what goes on at Mom's place, are you able to listen with interest, and not debate with them about what you think?

7. Have you got the skills and application to be all things (to your children) some of the time, as distinct from being some things to them all of the time—the warm and fuzzy, talking/feeling caregiver as well as the disciplinarian and authority figure?

8. Do you ever feel that you aren't going to be important to your kids if you don't have equal time? Could this be a reflection of how important you felt to them before separating?

9. Do you resent the idea of giving her money regularly, even if it is for the children, when she left you and got half of your hard-earned assets as well?

10. If you let out a critical or exasperated comment about her, do you accept that if the children hear it, half of their very being is being criticized?

11. Do you think you have an open, easygoing relationship with your kids so that if something was troubling them they could talk to you about it? Do you think if they wanted to change the shared arrangements in a way that resulted in them spending less time with you, they could bring this up?

12. If you have a new relationship that looks promising, are you prepared to adjust your plans for the new partnership if it could help the children's situation?

13. Do you find you prefer to be with the children with a girl-friend around or with your family and maybe their same-aged cousins?

14. Are you prepared to be doing things in an engaged way with your kids at their level fairly often or are you just as happy when they're doing things independently at arm's length?

How did it go? Pretty challenging? Hopefully you've now got a bit more of an idea about when you're doing things that aren't help-ful to your children and about what's really driving your attitudes toward your parenting responsibilities. Again, you should set aside some time to consider honestly how committed, child-focused, and compromising you are and possibly talk your thoughts through with a counselor.

· · · · ·

Jill says: It's important for parents to accept that feelings interfere and obscure important issues, but that they won't always. New partners are sometimes a great help with reality checks, though of course they can generate resentment and anxieties for some ex-partners. You have a responsibility to try to be child-focused and open-minded about your parenting role, which means letting go of pursuing fairness. You're not entitled to time with your children. They deserve and have a right to time with you. You won't be less important to your children just because they spend less time with you than your ex-partner.

Michael says: However valid your criticisms of each other are, you aren't going to safeguard your children from the influence of the things you dislike by making sure your children are with you half the time. It's sometimes difficult for a dad to be an emotional jack-of-

Q: My ex really indulges the children, even mollycoddles them. Surely this isn't good for them in the long term? Surely she should be a bit stricter with them? They don't seem willing to do much for themselves.

A: A lot of moms, in dedicated devotion to their children, probably do more running around for them than they need to. This can happen because they have the time to if they're not working, or because they're too busy to spend much time teaching the children self-sufficiency. (Doing it all themselves is quicker.) They may feel guilty about how much time they spend at work away from the family, so when they are with the children they don't want to be doing chores. Your children are living with two different regimes and you won't be able to influence hers much. That doesn't mean you can't gradually teach your children the rewards of contributing more to the daily round when they are with you, though they may need a lot of reminders about what you expect of them. Don't be tempted to tell her you think her way of parenting is wrong; you shouldn't need to assert to her your better parenting skills. But do tell her from time to time about things the children do independently that you're proud of. And don't feel that you must have equal time with them in order for your parenting ways to have a prominent influence on them.

all-trades. Young children especially want and need warm, patient, and communicative parenting which, at the risk of being sexist, is not something men are famous for! Shared parenting with young children means getting better at this feminine stuff, or you may find that your children crave for Mom and feel you don't understand.

• • • • •

KEY MESSAGES

- Shared parenting needs to be child focused, not adult centered.
- Check out your feelings about yourself, your ex-partner, and your kids—and be honest.
- Adult emotions can get in the way, especially if your ex-partner is in a new relationship.
- Being positive will help your children be honest about the arrangement.

six

Considering children's choices

I had my views about where I wanted to spend time, but
I didn't feel I could say anything about it to either of my
parents. I didn't want to be choosing between them. Even
now I'm older, if I drop in at Mom's work on the way home
from school in Dad's week to say "Hi" I sort of don't bother
to mention to him that I saw her. —*Sophie, 14*

How much you should involve your children in decision making
about shared parenting arrangements needs careful consideration.
They may have views that they express, and in some families where
everyone is getting on well—especially where there are older children—it is possible to have appropriate discussions involving everybody about how the separation is going to work or about reviewing
existing arrangements. Some research suggests that shared parenting is more likely to work when children are consulted and involved.
Yes, children do like to be consulted about things that concern and
affect them, but there are good reasons why care needs to be taken
here. Children are consulted today more than ever. We encourage
them to express themselves confidently and make decisions for
themselves. Sometimes they get their own way about things they're

really too young to decide on because today's parents are anxious to cultivate positive self-esteem and keen to be liked by their children. They equate firmness and direction with putting them down. In addition, many busy parents are time-poor, and may lack the time and effort that is necessary to be patient and authoritative with their children. Supporting children, encouraging them in healthy attitudes and principles, discouraging harmful ideas and behavior—all this takes time. A quick yes or no from a parent rushing off to work may work for the parent, but may not be good for the child.

Even if you pride yourself on running a fairly strict, traditional household, your kids are being schooled the modern way, which encourages healthy debate and questioning. They're growing up in a society that is democratic, where everyone has a right to have a voice. So attempts to be traditionally strict are likely to fail. There is confusion today about how to be an effective parent: you may be afraid to be firm, and proper parental authority (so important to children's security) can be easily eroded by children's energetic and often eloquent responses. Being separated is a further challenge to parental confidence at a time when major decisions requiring parental authority need to be made.

How much say should they have?

Our seemingly expressive and articulate kids can give the appearance of maturity. So we talk things through and ask their opinions as if their ideas and expressions are well thought out. But even older children need direction, even though they're often challenging the rules or expressing their views vigorously. Too much explaining and talking things through is often a sign of parental anxiety and a need for reassurance. As heads of the family, parents need to demonstrate courage and conviction, particularly when it comes to managing separation. Some kind of compromise is what's required in today's families, between giving in to your children—letting them make decisions *you* should be making—and hearing their input sympathetically while having the final say yourselves. Too little structure provided and too much self-determination granted too early makes for insecure and uncertain children.

> We'd had [the same] shared plan for several years. My ex wanted to review it because she said the kids weren't happy and that they wanted more time with her. I can talk with the kids about anything and they've never indicated to me that they wanted to be with me less. I think she wanted this really and maybe made them think they had to say it to her. —*Ken*

Divided loyalties

Parents, when feeling bad about putting their kids through a separation and anxious about their well-being, can put too much weight on what the children say and do. They can rely too much on seeking their children's views and enlisting their loyalties in order to get reassurance and approval for their own views and feelings. Separation divides children's loyalties. Each of them is half you and half your estranged partner, in character and temperament. If you encourage them, deliberately or otherwise, to express their preference for one kind of arrangement over another, you're really asking them to choose one parent over another. This is potentially damaging and will cause them to say what they think is safe and fair—not what they actually want—unless they feel confident that their parents are not competing with one another over them. But even if they aren't worried about how their views may affect their parents, they probably don't know whether what they think they want is actually what's best suited to their emotional needs.

Cooperative parents should be getting together and making these decisions for their children, at least at the start of a separation— certainly with younger children (say, under ten)—though much will depend on sibling configuration. (An only child of nine is in quite a different situation from a nine-year-old who is the youngest of four.) All the dilemmas and feelings associated with a changing family are confusing enough for us adults, so certainly what children think they want may be confused, changeable, and not well thought out. Keep in mind that children caught in loyalty conflicts quite often give distorted accounts to one parent of their experiences with the other—accounts that may seem significant to you but that are not always reliable indicators of feelings and preferences.

> My parents said I could please myself, but in a way I'd rather they'd told me what they wanted because I felt I always had to worry about their feelings and make sure I was spending about equal time with each of them just so as to be fair. I would be three or four days into a pleasant stay with Dad and I'd start worrying about whether it was soon going to be Mom's turn to have me. —*Dave, 12*

Children's wishes and the law

Lawyers often talk about a child's preference as if it is the deciding factor in resolving separation disputes. This tends to encourage parents to rely on, and even cultivate children's opinions and, as we've said, they may not be independent. In many, if not most, Western countries, the law is obliged to take into account children's wishes, particularly with older children, and judges do not ordinarily make orders that go against them. But the law usually has in place a system whereby children are assessed by psychologists who can independently interpret their wishes and give them the appropriate weight; this in turn is communicated to the court via an independent legal representative. (However, this only occurs in highly contentious cases; and a court is very unlikely to order a shared parenting agreement in this situation because in a case this factious, there is likely to be a lack of parental cooperation and/or an unwillingness to commit to a parenting plan.) Involving children in counseling and mediation is a relatively new idea, and we don't know much

Q: The children complain to me that they spend more time with Dad's family than with him, that he often uses his parents as babysitters. He wanted shared parenting but it seems only for someone else to do it for him. Isn't this unfair to them?

A: Are you sure they're really complaining? They mightn't mind all that much. You might resent it, but his family is important and may well be of great help to him as he gets used to his role in shared parenting. If you think he doesn't spend enough one-on-one time with them, you might be able to tactfully bring this up with him—perhaps during a general review—but if he hasn't worked this out for himself, you may not have much impact. Maybe his own father didn't do much hands-on parenting, and so he didn't grow up knowing how fathers engage with their kids, in which case he feels more comfortable being a step removed from hands-on connection. Perhaps this was the kind of father he was when you were together. In any case, at least your children know they are regularly in the company of their dad and his family rather than not there at all. It's important for separated fathers—who despite being dedicated dads have not played a hands-on role in their children's lives—to learn to do just that: to be with their children. This means arranging work so that they can spend time with them, not only going to movies or sporting events, but just hanging out, chatting, kicking around a ball, or cooking a meal together.

yet about the relationship between children's involvement in these processes and long-term outcomes. Our experience tells us—and studies in the United States confirm it—that children, as well as adults, benefit from programs that help them cope with the changes in their lives due to their parents' separation.

The likelihood is that your kids say different things to each of their parents, which may seem contradictory if not interpreted in their context. Of course, saying "I want to spend more time with you, Dad" doesn't necessarily mean "I want to spend less with Mom." Saying "I want equal time with each of you" doesn't mean that's actually what they want; it's what they think is fair to their parents, and it will enable them to avoid expressing a preference for one over the other. Your kids shouldn't have to be worrying about diplomacy and loyalties; they should be being kids, having fun, experimenting with life within safe boundaries, free from worries about their parents' difficulties.

This doesn't mean you shouldn't talk to and listen to what your children say. It does mean using those times as opportunities to reassure them that you're interested in what they have to say and are taking it into account, that you parents are going to take everything into account and sort out what's going to work.

> I campaigned to go and live with my father, saying to Mom that I needed to hang out with Dad more. He's less strict than Mom and seemed less worried about money. Eventually she agreed, and I was happy for a while, but I soon got a bit lonely as Dad in fact worked long hours and I was on my own a bit, which had seemed cool to begin with. Eating a lot of takeout was good at first, but it wasn't so "homey" at Dad's. —*Sean, 15*

How to involve your children in your parenting arrangement

You want your kids to feel as though they can talk with you honestly about how it's all going for them, without worrying that they might upset you. Invite them to review the arrangements from time to time. Children feel positive about shared arrangements with parents who are approachable and flexible, willing to change the way the days are shared, happy about children seeing their other parent outside the scheduled times, and able to encourage more independence about arrangements as they grow older.

If your own gut feeling combines with recurring expressions from the children to indicate that something about your arrangements needs changing, talk with your co-parent about it (more than once, preferably, to allow for careful consideration), before enlisting the children in negotiating anything. Keep in mind that it's likely they're saying quite different things to each of you from time to time.

Older children will naturally want to be more independent about their lives. If they want to have contact with their other parent during your time, don't be too rigid about it. They should be progressively taking charge of their own lives, which doesn't mean anything's changed in regards to how they feel about their parents!

> Flexibility is the important thing. The program cannot be static. You've got to adjust for the different ages of the children, the different things that happen. Kids change, you change, times change. If you allow for that, it will work well. —*Tom*

Some children's comments about sharing

Over the years we've heard parents expressing their range of emotions. But their children have strong feelings, too—of frustration, disappointment, confusion, loss. At the same time they demonstrate loyalty, empathy, adaptability, and resilience.

> Sometimes my mom says, "Do you want to change it and go for two weeks at a time so you have longer to settle in?" She thought I might be swapping over too often, but I reckon two weeks would be too long not to see each of them.

> When I go to Dad's for a few days he expects me to fit in as if I was always there. My room is really his office.

It's okay, but I prefer Mom's place even though it's farther from school and she works long hours. . . . It's a drag when you've got things at the wrong place. It was better when they organized for us to have a double set of everything.

My sister and I felt we had to hate Mom's boyfriend because he was with her before the separation, and Dad was outraged by this for years. Even after we felt okay about him we still acted like we didn't, to sort of protect Dad.

I prefer blocks of time, otherwise you're always thinking, where am I supposed to be tomorrow?

I'd really prefer more time at Mom's but I could never tell Dad.

Long after I left home I went on feeling I had to [call] Mom if I'd talked to Dad, or it wouldn't be fair.

I sometimes find I say things to Mom or to Dad that are a bit exaggerated. Like telling Mom it was boring at Dad's when it wasn't.

I'm a bit scared of Dad. I can't talk to him about things I can talk to Mom about, even though I've tried to. But then I certainly can't mention Dad's girlfriend to Mom, let alone that I quite like her!

I reckon having a week on/week off schedule is okay because we change over on Sunday night, and I see Dad at soccer practice during Mom's week. If I want to see Mom during Dad's week, he's cool about it.

When I left home, it was the nicest thing having all my gear in one place. I felt settled for the first time, after living out of a bag for years.

I wanted to spend more time with Dad when I was around fifteen, and I did. But whenever I talked to Mom on the phone, she made me feel I'd done the wrong thing by her. My feelings for her hadn't changed though.

The hardest thing about going back to Mom's was that she always wanted to know all about every detail of what we'd done together, who visited, whether Dad's girlfriend had stayed over and stuff, like I was supposed to be some sort of a spy!

· · · · ·

Jill says: Aim to do more listening to your children and less talking. Listen so you make them feel you've heard. If they want an answer, you don't have to give one immediately. Ask to talk about the issue again and see what they seem to be saying then. You don't always have to have the answers, either. Don't assume what they say is necessarily coming just from them, though it may be. Aim to be approachable and flexible.

Michael says: Being able to have meaningful conversations with children is an important part of being truly child focused. Small talk may seem to come more naturally to females, but fathers who aren't avid talkers can still learn how to contribute to conversations so they can connect to their kids. There doesn't always have to be an action plan or a decision at the end of a chat! Having parents who are approachable and open-minded about the idea of making changes as families grow and circumstances change makes children feel valued.

· · · · ·

KEY MESSAGES

- Children should have some say but not the final say.
- Understand that your children may have divided loyalties.
- Involve the children in parenting decisions with care.

seven

Working out a timetable

If you're cooperating flexibly with your partner and not worrying unduly about fairness, whatever division of time you have will be likely to work. As we've regularly asserted, contact with the father every other week is undoubtedly better than sporadic, halfhearted contact, but real parenting is more hands on than that arrangement allows. Fathers should seek and be encouraged to have much more time than the traditional two days out of fourteen. In fact, at least a third of their total time would be a better goal. It hasn't been established that children are confused or disadvantaged by having two places they call home; though many parents feel it must be, perhaps mainly because our ideal of traditional family life has centered on one home. But having two homes doesn't mean that hours and days must be divided evenly in order for each home to be emotionally significant for a child or for both parents to be important influences on their child.

> I was afraid that once we'd agreed on a plan I would never be able to change it. I wanted to start with four days [every two weeks] and build up slowly toward the children having more time with their dad, rather than start off with half-and-half. John was adamant that he was aiming to have equal

time eventually, which worried me a bit. But after several roundtable discussions, we arrived at a compromise with an undertaking to review. —*Isabelle*

Getting started

What guides your decisions in creating a parenting plan is likely to include all of these things: your passion about your children, money, geographical proximity, your children's ages, and your employment obligations. Try to regard plans as part of a process that needs to develop in phases as your children grow, allowing regular reviews.

With both parents spending substantial periods of time being responsible for their children, two homes are needed that can each shelter one parent and all the children comfortably. But just like equal hours spent in each home being overemphasized, it's another myth that the two homes have to be equally well-appointed for the children to have emotional stability (see also Chapter 2). Some parents feel that the children's stability will be preserved if they don't have to leave their familiar home as well as adjust to their parents' separating. Scheduling will be very affected by where the two of you live, and not just because of geography: if keeping the family home intact means one parent has to camp out in a much more modest place, it may be more difficult for the kids to adjust to feeling at home there. There are some advantages to both parents moving somewhere new, if it's all done with confidence and creativity. Children will adjust to leaving their past behind—if their parents can—in the same way that intact families adjust to relocation because of employment or other factors. This is because the parents have gotten the move sorted out for themselves and are being positive about it, celebrating it rather than grieving for the home they're leaving. After you've figured out your initial plans, you can put them into practice while you still all live together, if you can't move straight away—provided you can find a way to respect one another's authority and separateness with the children during each other's shift.

Separated parents should sit down with each other and analyze their lifestyles and what patterns exist for each family member. They should come up with a plan that they think might work and then present it to the kids, making whatever adjustments they think are necessary. They should be creative and, above all, positive about it. If they look at it with goodwill and confidence, the kids will pick up on that and it will work! Where there's a will there's a way!

> We were both determined not to let the kids suffer from our breakup. We resolved from the start that we would never fight in front of them and never say nasty things about each other. We decided on a program of contact and, with a few changes, have stuck to it. If we ever want to discuss some problem, we meet for coffee. —*Helen*

Scheduling patterns

Maybe a week-on/week-off arrangement will work, maybe a weekend plus some other days. If the parents live some distance from one another, perhaps trading off months is more appropriate. But continuity of schooling is important to all parents and children, and if parents have to move to accommodate this, then that's what should be done (if feasible). Wear and tear on everybody is minimized if there doesn't have to be too much regular commuting.

Even very young children can benefit from overnight stays with another parent. Overnight parenting makes for meaningful family experiences and should not necessarily be deferred just because children are young, so long as they are used to spending days and nights away from the parent who has been the primary caregiver, if indeed one parent had that role. If not, care and common sense should be exercised in gradually introducing an infant to this experience. The important principle here is that enjoyable time be spent frequently—with short intervals of a day or two between gradually increasing lengths of time—with the parent (usually Dad) who has had the less continuous, round-the-clock, caring role. Younger chil-

Q: Too much back-and-forth can be an extra stress, so shared residence is probably better in extended blocks, but how long with each parent is suitable?

A: It depends on the ages of your children. Week-on/week-off seems intuitively simple and conveniently predictable for many families, but you are the best judge of what stretches of time they can handle away from a particular parent. Consider a midweek interlude with whichever parent is off-duty. If that parent is attending sports practice and scheduled Saturday activities, whichever week it is, it helps children feel connected and gives a less sports-minded parent a break. So, once again, be creative! If geography is a factor and if the kids' relationships with both parents are well established and cooperative, longer periods will be quite okay with older children, but schooling and friendships will govern your decisions. Within similar educational systems, changing schools for a term or a year can be enriching for a confident child who is well supported by both parents.

dren as well as infants may be less comfortable with extended stays away from a parent, so breaking up time into slots of a few days rather than a whole week may work better.

School-aged children may have better continuity as far as school work goes if the same day of the week is spent with the same parent, though during the primary school years this is probably not so important.

We've always been flexible. We started off trading weekly, but changed to [every other week] when he went to high school. Then, in his final year, with all the study and pressure of exams, we thought it would be better for him to live in one spot, so he lived with me and visited his father a lot—that worked well. —Jo

Q: If it's a week-on/week-off arrangement, which is the best changeover day? Is it best if each parent is responsible for the same days of the week?

A: It depends on what your weekends involve. For pre-school children, it makes no difference, though it may for you. Sunday changeovers work well, allowing a chance to take stock and catch up before a new week. If Fridays are a family evening, then it makes this a good time to reconnect. Some families like the idea of the week at one home starting with a weekend so that the settling-in process is relaxed. Some parents find that having the same days of each week provides better continuity for school. If you miss all the dance classes because they're always on Tuesdays, then you can always go to the final performance. It's also more convenient for the dance teacher or the math tutor to deal with the same parent all the time.

Some parents have even tried "nesting," whereby they retain the family home for the children, and the parents move in and out according to a roster. The parents move about instead of the children, who stay in their established home. Like both parents setting up a new place at separation time, retaining the established home removes any feeling that the parent who left the home is the one who "left" the family, because the other parent still lives there with the children. This requires special parents who are willing to make special efforts to be so child focused. But it can work!

If there's goodwill and mutual support, this kind of dovetailing across designated parenting shifts keeps children and parents in touch with one another and actively demonstrates parental teamwork.

Other parents have found it useful to look first at the children's after-school activities—such as sports, music, or dancing—particu-

Q: It's the brief, everyday moments of family life that make you feel in touch with the kids. How can separated parents retain these contacts?

A: There's no reason why you shouldn't, say, pick up your son from Mom's and drop him at soccer practice on your off week, or pick him up and take him back as well. It helps Mom and it gives you those important windows with him. It needn't mean you are obliged to have a lot to do with Mom; you can just put it in your plan and it can happen like clockwork. And Mom could do the reverse when it's her off-week. If your job doesn't enable you to have much weekday contact with your child, why not drop by and take him to school?

larly for teenage children. Then they program their residential arrangements according to who can accompany or pick the kids up after regularly scheduled activities. In these cases, it may be that the boys can stay with Dad during football practice, and Mom can have some special time with the girls, or vice versa.

> It's a 5/2 formula: Mondays and Tuesdays, they are always with him; Wednesdays and Thursdays, always with me; and we alternate weekends. This gives continuity: the kids are in the same place for the same event and can keep the same gear in the same place. —*Julie*

There are all kinds of possibilities, and all of them workable, so long as the will is there to make them happen—and provided that both parents have a positive attitude about their parenting program. Too many changeovers and too much travel adds to everybody's burden. A simple arrangement helps everyone remember what's happening. Longer periods of time at one home, as children grow more able to do without one parent, allows for settling in to the routine of where they are before they have to change again.

> You've got to keep at it. There's no let-up—one kid's got to be here and the other somewhere else. One has forgotten his homework, and the other wants to see a friend. You've got to be really organized. But it's worth it. The kids haven't lost anything, and they are happy. We talk a lot. —*Gerry*

The key parenting plan principles

Your parenting plan will be built on three principles:

1. Your belief that your children need to feel valued and loved by both mother and father.
2. Your conviction that they need to belong to their community of parents, relatives, friends, schools, and favorite places.
3. Your intention to encourage one another to live happy, independent lives while being the best parents you can be.

Five examples of these principles in action

Plan one features two parents who both work, but have a certain amount of flexibility in their hours. The two girls, aged five and eight, have a week with Mom then a week with Dad, and change over on Sunday evenings. Because a week with one parent is quite a long time to go without seeing the other—especially for the five-year-old—they have Wednesday evenings overnight and go to school the next day with the off-duty parent in order to break up the week. This also gives each parent a mid-shift break.

Plan two involves a ten-year-old girl and fourteen-year-old boy who spend seven days with each parent in turn. Dad attends week-day sports practices every week. The on-duty parent sees the kids to school on a Monday, takes their belongings over to the other house, and the other parent starts their week with them after school on

Mondays. School holidays are pretty much the same, with parents reviewing them each year in advance if longer trips need to be fitted in.

Plan three incorporates alternating weeks and different blocks. The new shift begins on Sunday morning. For Dad Week 1 runs Sunday to Wednesday after school; in Week 2 it's Friday after school until Tuesday after piano lesson. This arrangement means that Dad is always responsible for the Sunday evening wind down before the school week, always deals with Monday homework (including math, which he can assist with), and does the Tuesday drop-offs to piano lessons. This means that each parent is responsible for the same days of the school week, giving consistency. During holidays they leave it the same unless they are going away. If a special school event occurs, both parents attend if available. If Mom wants a weekend out of town, she can ask for a Sunday from Dad (but not too often).

Plan four uses two-week blocks with each parent for two teenage girls who go to and from school independently. They make their own arrangements about contacting the parent. Mom works at a business near their school, so one of the girls often checks in on her way home. The changeover is on Friday night, so every other week begins with a weekend for settling in and catching up. They're beginning to organize holidays themselves depending on their parents' work commitments and their own plans.

Plan five has a nine-year-old boy who alternates weeks with his parents, changing over around the school day on Mondays. He attends school midway between his parents' residences but several suburbs away from each. He has tennis lessons after school, which take place nearby; he has a swimming class in Mom's neighborhood; and he attends a martial arts class in Dad's neighborhood. Although it's a fair drive for each parent to get him to school, this arrangement means that the boy's school community is no more associated with the mother's neighborhood than with the father's, so the parents feel of equal standing in their son's life.

I felt that I was giving away part of my motherhood. Some of my friends told me I was crazy and it was the wrong thing to do. But Dave was a good father and the kids missed him so much that I gave in, and now they are with him for five or six days every other week. I ached for them at first, but it's working out okay. I can do other things. The main thing is the kids are happy. —*Irene*

· · · · ·

Jill says: Parents should be creative in sorting out these arrangements, and be savvy about any protests or uncertainties coming from the children because they probably won't be all that coherently thought out. Rearranging the family is new ground for everyone in the family. Take time to consider the various possibilities before deciding on one.

Michael says: Not only must parents be creative, they should also be courageous. They have to put aside their fears and give it a go! They should be convinced that the effort is worth it and that the kids will quickly become used to the new system, particularly when they realize they are still seeing a lot of Mom and Dad, and others they have grown up with.

· · · · ·

KEY MESSAGES

- A timetable is always a work in progress.
- Get started by taking the time to analyze your lifestyles.
- Parenting arrangements can vary greatly.
- Consider the kids' schools and activities, your work, distances to travel, and so on, then sort out what best suits the family.
- Be creative, positive, and confident.

eight

Designing a parenting plan

I think it was quite good the way they had a proper written document about us. It made us feel they'd been really serious about us, and they met together several times to gradually work it out. Now we can refer to it if there are any disagreements. —*Andrew, 15*

Every family has a plan, whether it's written down or just worked out from time to time. Perhaps written parenting plans would be useful in intact families, too, but in a separated family they are extremely helpful, and sometimes essential. Not only does a good, documented plan prevent and solve disputes, it also makes life smooth and predictable. After separation, the lines of communication between parents, and between children and parents, are stretched. Living together in the same house made communication easy—arrangements could be made and changed in an instant. Geographical separation makes all that more difficult, calling for a different strategy. Even those parents who still talk to one another can't be on the phone every five minutes to change an appointment, to remind Dad to pick a child up after football practice, to tell Mom that vacation plans have to be changed.

Family life is complex enough. Parents work, full time and part time, and in separate locations. Children attend different schools

Q: I'm a bit uncertain about how much detail we need to have in a parenting plan. She has done most of the family homemaking things all these years and I'm happy for that to continue. Should we formalize things in writing?

A: You don't have to. But a separation is an important event in a family. However much trust and goodwill there is be-tween you, it's a good idea to sign off on family life as it was, and make a clear statement of how things are going to be from now on, even if it's a fairly general one. It's a com-mitted statement of the continuing responsibility you both intend to have for your children and how you're both going to express this involvement. And as time goes on, as circum-stances change, and new partnerships develop, your initial undertakings are on record as part of the family's history.

and have a variety of activities, each with its own schedule. As kids grow up their needs change. Separated family life is even more com-plex. The best idea is, therefore, to make it as easy as possible. This is what a written parenting plan will do for you.

Your own parenting plan

You can set down in black and white all the things that you both agree are important for looking after yourselves and your children from now on. Your parenting plan is yours. Have a look at the sample parenting plans in Chapter 9, but don't feel limited in any way. Your plan can contain as much or as little detail as you decide is necessary to make it work. It can include your philosophy of parenting, your attitudes toward your children's well-being, the particular needs of each of the children, plans for schools and future education, details about medical care, where each parent will live, a schedule of the children's living arrangements, transportation, holidays, religious events, special festive days—even legal issues if you wish. Take some time on this: exchange drafts, think about it, get some advice if you think you need it, and then formalize it with your signatures.

What to include in your parenting plan

A plan might contain some or all of the following elements:

- The parents' philosophy and attitudes regarding their care of the children
- An acknowledgment of responsibilities for the welfare of the children
- Daily decisions and more major ones that require consultation
- Where everyone will live
- What time or times the children will spend with each parent, grandparents, and so on
- The importance of maintaining relationships with parents and others
- How the travel between homes will occur
- The schools, school activities, and extracurricular programs
- Arrangements for vacations, holidays, and other special days
- Special needs regarding medication, education, clothes, or equipment
- Financial arrangements, including extra expenses
- Communication between the two parents and sharing information about the children
- Communication between the parents and the children via telephone, email, and so on
- Appointment of a mediator/coordinator to deal with disputes
- A specified time for a review of the plan
- Additional agreements, for example, not to discuss money in the presence of children, and so on

It was all our own work. We had friends already doing shared parenting and we thought it was the way to go. We are convinced it's advantageous for the kids—they're not bargaining chips, and they need to know that both parents want them. We find alternating weeks works well, with the changeover Sunday evening. The parent without the kids picks them up (so they won't feel one parent is getting rid of them). —*Brian*

Collaborative parenting plans

This is the type of plan that will work for separated parents who can treat one another with decency and sensitivity, who acknowledge the importance of both parents in the children's lives, and who work hard to foster all the relationships that are important for their children. They talk to one another regularly about the children. Their children's friends are welcome in either home. In some cases they are able to come together for Christmas and birthday parties and the like. Many separated parents are doing this!

But no matter how well you are getting on with your ex-partner, a written parenting plan is still a valuable asset. Even in the most amicable of separated households, accidents and misunderstandings arise. People are different and sometimes difficult, and the same goes for children. Circumstances can change; unexpected things happen. The separated family is a special family, and living in it calls for a special effort. At times it's easy for the best of parents to tire, to lose heart, to feel exhausted, to wonder if their efforts are worthwhile.

A well-constructed and principled parenting plan can help you through the tough times. You can take it out and read it again. You can discuss it with your ex-partner or your children. It will help you renew your commitment and may help renew your enthusiasm. One of the key features of a collaborative parenting plan is the commitment of both parents to consult one another on issues that affect the children, their welfare and development.

Q: I'm finding what to do about the children's arrangements incredibly difficult to deal with. I feel so upset for them. I don't trust their father to do the right thing by them. I don't want to have anything to do with him. I don't want them staying overnight with his girlfriend there, and I want him to feed them properly and stick to sensible bedtimes. Can I have all this put in a parenting plan?

A: You can have very specific details incorporated into your plan, and so can he. There's no limit to what you can have included. If you feel he's out of touch with their routines, inform him, perhaps with the help of a mediator if talking with him is very uncomfortable for you. You could also write lists for him, as appendices to a parenting plan. For the period while everyone gets used to the separation, you could suggest that he spend his time with them without his partner. Try to approach the creation of your plan with an open mind, inviting him to draw up as many clauses as he wants to. Work out yourself what sort of issues you want to be consulted on, and aim to set out the arrangements very specifically so you don't need to have much contact with him. You may be well advised to have a neutral third party as a pick-up and drop-off person, so you don't have to see him, and the children don't sense your discomfort.

We told our lawyers what we wanted and they were really good. They helped us work through all the things that we thought were needed to make life easy for the children. They also made some good suggestions. After a couple of sessions, we signed a parenting agreement and they filed Consent Orders in the court. —*Sarah*

Parallel parenting plans

For parents who find it impossible to get along, parallel parenting can work. That means each household has its own set of rules, and the parents have a minimum of contact and communication. The one thing that they agree on is that the children have two parents and that they are going to spend some time in each household according to a determined schedule.

The essential ingredient in such a plan is the commitment of both parents to stick to the terms of their agreement. Moreover, the plan will need to be extremely detailed to cope not only with the children's day-to-day timetables, but also to foresee and deal with expected changes and hiccups.

Where there is ongoing hostility between separated parents and little or no communication, a written parenting plan is essential. With it, and with a firm commitment to abide by the rules, shared parenting can still work. Without it, misunderstandings and confusion will inevitably arise and children will suffer.

> I've found that the best way to deal with a difficult decision is to WRITE IT DOWN, and then ask myself: how is this going to affect the kids? How is it going to affect my ex-wife? How will it affect me? This has stopped me from doing some very stupid things. —Jim

Sure, there will be problems, even after implementing the most carefully structured parenting plan. Life's like that! Life is never smooth or uneventful, whether your family is intact or separated. Why should it be? Human beings—including children—and human events are naturally unpredictable and, at times, quite unreliable. People react in different ways to similar circumstances. If it were any different, life and people would be deadly dull and boring.

Making what's best for the kids work for parents, too

COMMUNICATE

Make sure everything goes from parent to parent, not through the kids. Use the phone, email, or a contact book, if necessary, to avoid confrontation or debate in front of the children. (See Chapter 10.)

COOPERATE

You and your ex-partner no longer have to agree over who washes the dishes, but you need to agree—or at least agree to disagree—when it comes to the kids. If necessary, have separate rules at each household and respect the differences. Kids will adjust so long as each parent is consistent.

KEEP ROLES CLEAR

Remember: (s)he's no longer your spouse, but (s)he will always be your child's parent. Perspective counts when trying to cool easily inflamed emotions.

GET A GO-BETWEEN

If matters get out of hand, enlist a mediator or specialized counselor to defuse tension and to resolve disputes.

Flexibility

If your parenting is going to work, you have to build into your plan an element of flexibility to cater for those occasions when something just cannot happen; or, if it's already happened, that calls for a change in plans. Be flexible about demanding makeup time. But, more importantly, you have to build into *yourself* an element of flexibility, of give-and-take. You have to tell yourself that life is not always smooth sailing and easy. It is not so in intact families, so why should it be in separated families? Chill out, settle down, and don't expect too much of yourself, your ex-partner, or the children. Be positive and do your best: it will surely get easier.

> We've had a shared arrangement going for several years. I guess you could call it "parallel" as we don't talk much and are very different. Both of us have weekday time with the kids, and I think it's important to be involved in their schoolwork as I'm a bit stricter than their mom. When she wanted to move to the other side of town, we weren't able to work out a compromise because we'd never been able to talk, and I didn't want to give up my weekdays. I was happy for her to move, but not take the children. —Jim

You may want to formalize your parenting plan and make it legally binding. This may make you feel safer and more signed off. It means that if your ex-partner does not abide by the terms of the agreement you can file an application in court. In most jurisdictions, you must have your plan written in the form of a legal document so it can be lodged as Consent Orders in the appropriate court. But of course this still allows you to vary the orders by mutual agreement without having to go back to court.

Examples of both collaborative and parallel parenting plans are set out in Chapter 9. You'll note that there is little difference in the essential elements of each kind of plan. But in the parallel plan you will see less warm language and a stronger emphasis on sticking to the rules and to appointing a really good coordinator. The promise to attend a parenting program is particularly important in parallel parenting situations. If nothing more, separated parents who do not communicate with one another should see the parenting plan as a means of making life easy and reducing unpleasantness.

• • • • •

Jill says: It's sometimes assumed that parenting can't be shared unless Mom and Dad are communicative and cooperative. Obviously, parents getting on well is ideal, but parallel parenting can mean shared parenting is possible with minimal communication and with different parenting styles. Children can cope with distance and minimum communication between their parents, provided everything's sorted out, set down, and adhered to.

Michael says: The great value in committing your arrangements to paper is that it sets out in black and white your commitment as decent and sensible parents to look after your children and yourselves after the breakup of your marriage. It tells your children and the world that you're taking this seriously and that you're going to measure up to the responsibilities that parenthood brings. It proclaims your belief that your separation does not represent a tragic failure and that family life is finished. Rather, it announces your firm intention to care for your children while getting on with your own lives.

• • • • •

KEY MESSAGES

- Every family needs to commit to a plan.
- Your plan can include all the details you each need.
- Collaborative parenting plans are for parents who can talk to one another.
- Parallel parenting plans are for those who find communication difficult.
- What works for the kids will work for the parents.
- Above all, be flexible.
- If you wish, you can formalize your plan at court.

nine

Sample parenting plans

Here are some sample parenting plans to show the range of detail possible. It's up to you to negotiate what you want in yours.

Sample collaborative parenting plans

Collaborative Parenting Plan A

This is a fairly simple one, suitable when the child is an infant and where there is reasonable communication and collaboration between parents.

The following is the agreement reached between John and Liz Smith in December 2005, concerning the shared parenting arrangements for their daughter Jane (aged 18 months):

. . . .

John and Liz will share the responsibility for Jane equally.

Her time is to be spent substantially in the care of her mother, with liberal time spent with her father commensurate with her age and emotional development.

In the immediate term this will operate with Jane spending each Tuesday evening from approximately 6 p.m. in her father's care, overnight until Wednesday morning.

On alternating weeks she will in Week 1 spend Thursday evenings with her father from approximately 6 p.m. until 8.30 p.m. or when she is put to bed by him at her mother's home; and Saturday overnight, commencing Saturday afternoon and extending into Sunday as agreed.

In the following week (Week 2), the Thursday night as described above will be substituted by Friday overnight, and the very next Sunday she will spend the evening with her father from around 6 p.m. until her bedtime at her mother's home.

	M	T	W	T	F	S	S
Wk 1		overnight		eve		overnight	
Wk 2		overnight			overnight		eve

Until further notice, neither parent will have Jane in their sole care for vacations longer than a few days without contact with the other parent.

Christmas, Easter, and other holidays are to be shared reasonably as agreed.

The above arrangements can be varied from time to time if agreed upon and do not exclude John seeing Jane at other times should he seek to do this.

Signed and Dated: _____

. . . .

Comment: The first two clauses express the basic principle of the plan; then "liberal" time with John is defined across a two-week period in a way that spreads his time with Jane at regular intervals so they never have a very long period between contacts and so Jane doesn't have any long periods away from her mother. This is appropriate for such a young child whose parents have both been involved in her overnight routines.

Collaborative Parenting Plan B

Here there are three children under 10, the youngest an infant. The mother had initiated the separation and in the short term agreed to leave the home except for the purposes of parenting.

In February 2006, Fran and David Brown met twice with mediator Joan Settlewell and the following was proposed:

The three children remain residing at the family home.

David continues to reside there and be primarily responsible for the children on weekdays when school is in session from 7 p.m. until 7 a.m.

Fran will no longer reside there but will have access to it from 7 a.m. until 7 p.m. on weekdays when school is in session and be primarily responsible for the children during these times (see below). In the event of both parents being there at the same time, then responsibility for the children will be joint.

A room will be maintained for use by Fran for the purposes of assisting overnight when agreed.

Fran and David will plan how the weekends are allocated and agree on some minimum numbers of weekends each, having in mind that it be as equal as possible. Fran's weekend contact will take place with the children's residence as a base, with outings arranged by her and overnight stays elsewhere, as arranged, until such time that Fran sets up suitable premises of her own where the children can stay for weekends and holidays.

School holidays will be shared as agreed. Every effort will be made to give each other as much notice as possible about plans for holidays.

Both Fran and David will seek the other's assistance first when childcare is necessary during their periods of responsibility.

Both Fran and David undertake to keep one another informed of activities and excursions involving the children so as to keep one another reasonably in touch with the children.

Fran and David will have joint responsibility, consulting each other on decisions about the long-term care, welfare, and development of the children, including but not limited to all aspects of their education, health, sports, religious attendance or training, and any plans for interstate or overseas travel.

Fran will have sole responsibility for making decisions about the day-to-day care and welfare of the children during the periods they are in her care.

David will have sole responsibility for making decisions about the day-to-day care and welfare of the children during the periods they are in his care.

This parenting plan is to be implemented as soon as practicable after Fran and the children return from their forthcoming extended vacation, and is to be reviewed six months later. In the event of significant circumstances changing before this review, it may be brought forward. These circumstances may include, for example, David finding a new partner, the house being sold, or Fran taking up employment.

If disputes arise, Fran and David undertake to settle them quickly and with the help of a mediator if necessary.

Signed and Dated: _____

. . . .

Comment: This plan recognizes that Fran was the instigator of the separation, that David was quite resentful of Fran's decision, and both parents were very keen not to unsettle the children more than necessary. He wanted some specific undertakings in the agreement in order to feel comfortable, which Fran was quite happy to give, even though she didn't feel she particularly needed them in there. David worked during the day but Fran at this stage didn't, so their day and night shift arrangement made common sense. You'll see that there are two paragraphs toward the end that define Fran and David's decision-making responsibilities. This makes a clear, almost formal, statement of committed intention, which is often helpful. The mention of the mediator was something they decided to put in because it was going to remind them of how they arrived at the decision—that a professional third party had assisted them and thereby endorsed the agreement.

Collaborative Parenting Plan C

This one concerns two primary-aged children. The mother works part-time and the father works full-time. The father is very anxious to have half time and the mother is very concerned about the kids having so much time away from her.

The following parenting arrangements and undertakings were agreed upon in July 2004:

Julie and Simon will continue to have shared responsibility for their children, Jack and Sophie, and honor the principle of meeting their need to be with each of their parents for as much time as possible, having regard to their other needs as they grow and develop.

The children will be in the care of Simon in Week "A" from Monday afternoon until Wednesday morning, when Julie takes over their care until Friday afternoon/early evening. Simon then has them for the weekend (beginning Friday) and until Tuesday of Week "B," when Julie has them from the Tuesday afternoon until the following Monday.

Julie and Simon will remain committed to a principle of flexibility to accommodate their respective commitments, for work or otherwise. To honor the principle of the children being with their parents in preference to other caregivers, each will call upon the other to assist with the children during their periods of responsibility, as deemed appropriate.

Julie and Simon will have joint responsibility, consulting with each other on decisions about the long-term care, welfare, and development of the children, including but not limited to all aspects of their education, health, sports, religious attendance or training, and any plans for interstate or overseas travel.

Julie will have sole responsibility for making decisions about the day-to-day care and welfare of the children during the periods they are in her care.

Simon will have sole responsibility for making decisions about the day-to-day care and welfare of the children during the periods they are in his care.

It is agreed that parenting arrangements will be reviewed quarterly, or at the request of either Julie or Simon.

Julie Jones _____

Simon Smith _____

Agreed this date _____

....

Comment: Simon really wanted a week-on/week-off arrangement, but recognizing that Julie thought a week without contact with one of the parents was too long, they broke the week up into shorter segments, describing the weeks as "A" and "B." There isn't anything particularly recommendable about planning in two-week cycles, it's just that alternating is easier to remember and has a manageable rhythm to it. Julie and Simon wanted quarterly reviews, and you'll note that either can request a review at any time. This is important, as even if one parent thinks everything's fine and doesn't see the need for a review, if the other does see this need, then there should be a review. They are still partners for the purpose of committed co-parenting.

Collaborative Parenting Plan D

This plan for Tom (11) and Kate (9) utilizes the established nanny, Sharon, who works in both homes, providing some useful continuity.

This is the parenting agreement between Jackie and Mike mediated in October 2005. It is based on the underlying principle that Jackie and Mike continue to have joint and equal rights and responsibilities in relation to the children, Tom and Kate, and that neither parent wishes in any way to be less involved or associated with the children than previously, while recognizing that spending less actual time with the children is the inevitable consequence of the separation.

Without prejudice to the future, and with the understanding that these arrangements are initial arrangements for the immediate term pending review, the following agreement is proposed.

- The children reside with Jackie from Monday after school through Thursday, Sharon assisting
- On alternate weeks from Thursday after school until Monday morning, the children reside with Mike at his premises with the assistance of Sharon on Thursdays and Fridays
- On the intervening weekend, the children continue in the care of Jackie from Thursday until Sunday afternoon at around 5 p.m. or as otherwise agreed, when they go to Mike's where they stay overnight until school the next morning

- Both Mike and Jackie have contact with the children during their time with the other parent as agreed for events such as basketball, and so on.
- When either Mike or Jackie travels on business, the children are in the care of the other parent and return to the care of the traveling parent upon return, making the necessary adjustment to the alternating routines.

During school holidays the children are to remain in their father's care on his weekends until Tuesday, or to commence their weekend with him on Wednesday, and at such other times during the school holidays as agreed.

Neither parent is to make plans to move anywhere with the children to a distance that would affect shared parenting significantly without consultative, cooperative, open discussion about the implications of a contemplated move.

The arrangements are to be reviewed (with the assistance of the mediator if sought by either), at least when the new year's calendar is set and commitments are known, or sooner if necessary.

Signed and Dated _____

. . . .

Comment: This plan begins with an overall statement of commitment, which often feels good to have in writing. The hardest part of making a plan is often getting the arrangement started. Parents get anxious about setting precedents, or worry that they won't be able to change things once they've agreed to them. Hence the "without prejudice" clause. Parenting plans, of course, are about children, who grow and change all the time, so there should be a set of arrangements to get started, which can easily be adjusted once it's been tried out. Sometimes it helps to specify school days and holiday times separately, as Mike and Jackie have done here. Note also the undertaking about possible relocation by either of them.

Sample parallel parenting plans

These are useful where there is little communication and collaboration, and arrangements have to be nailed down. They can also be used for collaborative parents who like a lot of detail.

Parallel Parenting Plan A

Names _____

We, Mike and Tracy, are the parents of _____.

1. General principles

Although we have chosen to live together no longer, we will both continue to be active and involved parents to our children. We have generally agreed in principle on parenting issues and intend our parenting to remain cooperative, united, and consistent as far as possible in the circumstances.

We also believe that, as well as being our desire, it is in the best interests of our children that they have close and loving relationships with both of us. We agree on this:

* We are both competent, trustworthy and loving parents.
* We are both responsible for the parenting of our children. Irrespective of where the children are living, we both have a responsibility and a right to participate in significant parenting decisions, and agree to regularly consult each other and keep each other informed about parenting issues.
* We will endeavor to maintain a friendly relationship between us.

2. Naming

Our children are named Ben and Isabel, and are to be known by these names. Each of us will refer to the other as the children's mother or father. We will not encourage the children to call any other person mother or father.

3. Shared parenting

We agree to the following:

- Consistently acknowledge and promote the special role that each of us has in the lives of our children
- Regularly discuss the children's progress regarding their intellectual, emotional, and physical development
- As far as is possible and practicable, to consult each other regarding the children's routines, discipline, schooling, clothes, health, and welfare
- Seek and value the children's wishes regarding these shared parenting arrangements and act on these, taking into account what is appropriate considering the children's ages

4. Health and emotional well-being

We will foster good health and emotional well-being in our children. To ensure this we will do the following:

- Make joint decisions about our children's health and emotional well-being
- Agree not to denigrate each other and endeavor to maintain a friendly relationship between us
- Agree not to denigrate each other's interests and associations and to deal respectfully with other cultures, particularly in relation to the children
- As far as possible keep the children to their normal routines with regard to bedtimes, sleeping arrangements, clothing, and general well-being
- Ensure that our children's milestones (for example, birthdays) are acknowledged wherever they are living
- Whenever possible, both attend celebrations and special occasions such as school presentations and sporting events
- Keep each other informed about our children's emotional and physical health

- Inform those who are entrusted with the care, education, or treatment of our children of any important medical information
- Cooperate with any remedial intervention recommended by a competent health professional

5. Discipline

We agree to discuss and review the children's behavior and any possible disciplinary action. We agree not to use physical discipline (hitting), humiliation, or shaming, and we will ensure that anyone else to whom we entrust the care of the children will also abide by this.

6. Residence arrangements

To facilitate shared parenting, we agree to live within 30 minutes' travel of the children's school. We agree that the parent in whose home the children will live will collect the children from the other's residence. Residence arrangements will take into account weekends with each parent and the midweek activities of the children. The following plan shall commence on May 2, 2010:

During Week 1, the children will live with their mother from Friday after school to Monday morning. The father will pick up the children from school on Monday and they will live with him until the following Monday morning.

During Week 2, the children will live with their mother from Monday after school until Friday morning. The father will pick up the children from school and they will live with him until Monday morning.

During Week 3, the children will live with their mother from Monday after school until the following Monday morning.

During Week 4, the children will live with their father from Monday after school until the following Friday morning.

This pattern will continue throughout the year unless changed by agreement. Otherwise times will occur as agreed between the parents. On Christmas Day, birthdays, Mothers' and Fathers' Days, the children will spend at least part of those days with each parent. Each parent may telephone the children at any convenient time within reason. Each parent will participate in the children's school activities, which may include reasonable contact at the school with the children.

We also agree that we will advise each other of any proposed travel or overnight visits outside the usual residential arrangements. The parent with whom the children are living on any day is responsible for their care if they are sick or during school or public holidays. That parent is also responsible for supervising homework and other school-related activities and extracurricular activities.

If either parent is unable to care for the children for a period of more than 48 hours, the other parent will be notified immediately so that we might agree on appropriate care for the children. The children can phone the other parent at any time and vice versa (within reason). We will not make any plans for holidays outside the normal residence arrangements without gaining the other parent's consent. We will inform each other of any vacation plans in advance, with suitable details such as travel times, contact phone numbers, and so on.

7. Education

We will ensure that we provide the best possible educational opportunities for our children and encourage them to pursue their special interests. We will supervise and support homework and practice.

Each parent has the right to participate in activities and receive information regarding our children's education, irrespective of which parent is caring for the children at the time of any school activities. We will pass on to each other any information we receive about our children's education.

8. Family relationships

We agree to foster close relationships between the children and their immediate and extended families by arranging regular visits and telephone contact.

9. Child support

We agree that we will share equitably in the costs of raising our children and that we will jointly make financial decisions about our children whether or not we each contribute equally in financial terms to their support.

10. Death of parents

We agree that, in the event of the death or incapacity of one of us, the other parent will assume full responsibility for the care, welfare, and development of our children. We both agree to bequeath to the children a sufficient proportion of our estates to ensure that their living and educational costs can be met until they become adults.

11. Communication, consultation, information sharing, and conflict resolution

We agree to the following:

- Share as much information about our children as possible in the circumstances
- Share information with our children to ensure that, as far as practical and in an age-appropriate way, they remain reassured that the separation of their parents has not diminished our relationship with them and that they are not left insecure about the future; we acknowledge the children's right to know about changes in family relationships and the desirability of involving them in decisions that will affect them, such as proposed changes to living arrangements, introduction of new partners, and so on
- Resolve conflict constructively, cooperatively, and in the best interests of our children. If we experience a conflict over the

parenting of our children that we cannot resolve ourselves, we will seek counseling or mediation to resolve the issue

12. Reevaluation of the parenting plan

We agree to review this parenting plan as a matter of course, in June of each year, until we decide this is no longer required. We will also review the plan at any other time as our children's needs and/or circumstances change, as our needs as parents and/or circumstances change, or at the request of either of us, or the children. For example, we would review the plan before either of us changes residences, if either of us re-partners, if another child is born, after a family crisis or death, or when each child completes primary school.

13. Acceptance

We acknowledge that we need to implement the parenting plan in both practice and spirit for the well-being of our children and ourselves. We have each carefully considered the provisions contained in the parenting plan, and exercise our informed choice by signing it. We agree that we will each keep a copy of the parenting plan.

Name _____

Name _____

Signature _____

Signature _____

Date _____

Date _____

Comment: You can see that there are undertakings about proper parenting principles spelled out in many of the sections of this plan. It can help very estranged parents who are suspicious and distrusting of one another to have these written down in detail. There's quite a lot of detail in the thirteen sections, and residence is set out in a four-week cycle with changeovers around the school day, which is preferable when parents are uncomfortable with each other. The cycle continues throughout the year regardless of school holidays. Even the review clause has specific reasons set out in detail. The principle of having so many details spelled out is that it means very little has to be discussed—it's all in there.

Parallel Parenting Plan B

This parenting plan is a formal statement by Jack and Kathie of how the needs of Lilly are going to be met after the separation and divorce of her parents.

....

This parenting agreement covers the following important areas:

1. Residential and childcare arrangements
2. Time spent with each parent and the wider family
3. Recreation and holiday arrangements
4. Resolution of conflict
5. Education and religion
6. Health and medical issues
7. Parental responsibilities
8. Relocation of residence
9. Process to alter the agreement

The aims of this agreement are as follows:

• To make residential and other provisions for Lilly that encourage each parent to maintain a loving, stable, and nurturing relationship with Lilly, consistent with her developmental level and the family's social and economic circumstances

• To ensure that Lilly spends ample time with both parents so as to allow her to develop a meaningful, not a superficial, relationship with her mother and father and others important to her upbringing

- To promote the amicable settlement of disputes between Jack and Kathie, which will enhance the well-being and stability of Lilly

Objectives

- To provide for Lilly's physical care
- To maintain Lilly's emotional stability
- To provide for Lilly's changing needs as she grows and matures
- To set out the authority and responsibilities of each parent with respect to Lilly
- To minimize Lilly's exposure to harmful parental conflict
- To encourage both Jack and Kathie to meet their responsibilities to Lilly through this parenting agreement, rather than by relying on judicial intervention
- To otherwise protect the best interests of Lilly
- It is agreed that because individuals' lives and children's developmental needs continually change, this agreement must be flexible and allow room for adjustment

A definition of shared parenting

It is the intention of the parents who have agreed to shared parenting that each of them shall continue to have a full and active role in providing a sound social, economic, educational, and moral environment for Lilly. The parents agree to consult with one another on substantial questions relating to educational programs, religious upbringing, significant changes in social environment, and health care. They agree to exert their best efforts to work cooperatively in making plans consistent with the best interests of Lilly and in amicably resolving disputes as they arise, without involving Lilly.

1. Residential and childcare arrangements

- Lilly will live for one week with her mother and for the following week with her father.
- Changeover day shall be every Wednesday, unless varied by agreement.

- The parent who is to have care of Lilly for the week shall pick her up from school on Wednesday afternoon and take her back to school the following Wednesday morning.

2. Time spent with each parent and the wider family

Whenever Lilly's grandparents, uncles, aunts, cousins, and so on are visiting, Lilly is to be afforded all reasonable opportunity to spend time with them at the residence of the parent in question, so that she might get to know her extended family. It is agreed that reasonable account will be taken of the total time spent with that particular parent.

3. Recreation and holiday arrangements

Lilly is to enjoy alternate Christmases with each of her parents, with this year being a Christmas spent with her father. School holidays shall be shared, or the normal program adhered to, after consultation between the parents. Lilly is to be able to have free, unhindered telephone contact with both her parents. Both parents agree to encouraging and enabling such contact to work so that it can become meaningful and free from tension for Lilly.

4. Resolution of conflict

If disputes or conflict arise, the parents agree to settle these as quickly as possible and without involving Lilly. They will first attempt to resolve disputes between themselves, but failing this, agree to seek mediation with the nearest available agency.

5. Education and religion

Both parents agree to bring up Lilly with the values and principles of their religion. The choice of school and religion is to be discussed and mutually agreed upon by both parents. Both parents will together make the choice of school and any other major decisions for Lilly. In the event of disagreement, then the provisions made for mediation will apply. Both parents will endeavor to negotiate with a spirit of resolution rather than conflict, and to arrive at an outcome with the best interests of Lilly in mind. The school is to be notified of this parenting agreement, and in the event of any serious problem or accident at school, both parents are to be notified. All reports and any information on any school activities or invitations will be sent to both parents; both parents will have an equal right to discuss any issues with the school authorities; and neither will be prevented from being involved. Both parents will discuss and come to agreement on any such issues together before making any decisions.

6. Health and medical issues

The parent having actual physical custody of Lilly at any point in time shall take responsibility for dealing with medical and dental emergencies. Both parents agree to discuss the general health care needs of Lilly and to advise each other of illnesses and treatment requirements. Any other health issues are to be discussed and mutually agreed upon.

7. Parental responsibilities

It shall be the responsibility of both parents to prevent any form of parental alienation, and neither parent will put down the other parent in front of Lilly, but rather assure her that both parents love her and care for her.

8. Relocation of residence

If either parent desires to move out of the area, the parents must discuss this in advance and adjust the shared parenting agreement accordingly.

9. Process to alter the agreement

Lilly's parents promise to make genuine attempts to implement and adhere to this agreement for Lilly. Should one parent consider that any change or alteration is necessary, that parent shall immediately contact the other and discuss the situation.

Signed _____ Mother

Signed _____ Father

Comment: This plan starts out with quite a lot of introductory material: a statement of what the plan covers, its objectives, and even a definition of shared parenting. As we noted earlier, these formal statements can provide nervous or resentful parents with reassuring reference points. Note the undertaking to provide Lilly's school with a copy of the plan. Also, there is no obligation to refer to the other parent for assistance with Lilly's care in their time with her. The cooperative dovetailing, which appeared in many of the cooperative parenting plans, doesn't work with estranged parents, who will be communicating minimally with each other and not needing to know too much about the other's lives, such as how often they use babysitters.

· · · · ·

Jill and Michael say: Remember, you can have as much or as little detail in your parenting plan as you like. The more detail you have in it, the less need there is to consult each other—you both know what's happening.

· · · · ·

ten

Communicating between households

Throughout this book we've stressed the importance of talking to each other about planning your arrangements and managing your parenting responsibilities. Once you've got your shared arrangements up and running, how much communicating is necessary and how can it be improved for the sake of harmony and cooperation? What can parents do in their conversations with their children to help? First we'll address the issue of consulting between parents.

> They never said anything to us for ages, but we knew. And when they eventually sat us down, they thought we'd be surprised and shocked. We'd been expecting it. We'd overheard them talking about breaking up. It was kind of a relief to have it more in the open now, but I still don't talk about it to them. —*Matt, 8*

Between parents

The emotional turmoil of separating parents means that difficult feelings interfere with sensible parenting. Sometimes parents just split up and allow things to happen. They don't sit down as a family and tell their children what's going on. And how does this situation unfold? The kids find out in fits and starts, getting differing and contrasting messages from their parents, their friends, and relations. These parents don't give their children clear answers to questions about where they'll live, what's going to happen, and why. They fail to reassure their children of their continuing love and involvement.

A good start is when parents both shoulder the responsibility for what's happening (regardless of who they might feel is more to blame for damaging the relationship) and take positive steps to make it work. This means having many conversations together over a period of time about all the different possible arrangements that might be good for you and your children, and about what you're going to say to them about why you're separating. You're aiming to make a concerted effort to start having different conversations with your partner now—as fledgling co-parents, no longer as frustrated lovers. And you're aiming to retain your joint position at the head of the family despite separating.

> We hardly ever saw each other. We emailed important news and information. If I wanted to make a change in the arrangements, it just wasn't worth the angst, so I always stuck to the letter. Sometimes if there was a school function Tom would ask if only one of us, not both, could go. This was sad, but I guess it was easiest for him this way. One day, I hope things will relax a bit more, but for the time being it seems to be working all right with us at arm's length, and for me personally, it's easier. —*Fran*

Hints for difficult discussions

- Recognize that your concern for your children arouses very strong feelings and sensitive reactions.
- Set aside a time (an hour maximum) when there's unlikely to be any interruptions. Agree on this appointment in advance to allow you each to prepare thoughtfully.

- Choose neutral territory—a café or park.
- Agree that there are going to be several of these planning meetings because this is not only very important, it's also going to be very difficult.
- Set some ground rules together about the length of the meeting, about reserving the right to adjourn if there's a stalemate or if one of you gets too emotional to talk coherently, or to allow thinking time. Acknowledge that any viewpoint expressed or proposal made is provisional and can be withdrawn, altered, or added to.
- Don't feel you've always got to respond to your partner straight away. You can keep charge of the pace (and therefore the intensity) of your discussions if you pause and say you're going to think about that proposition or claim, and reply in due course.
- Try to summarize where you've left the issues discussed in terms of who's proposed what, what's agreed, what's not agreed, what you're going to do prior to the next discussion, and so on.

> There are days when I want to just scream from the rooftops, "How did this happen, and why?" I've become a master at learning how to count to ten when I get angry. But I don't have much choice but to behave with as much integrity and strength of character as I can, because even though the marriage has failed, we can make the divorce succeed, especially where the children are concerned. —Karl

If your meetings break down

If the two of you can't communicate productively, consider seeing a separation counselor or divorce mediator together. If you don't know what's going to be best for your children, see a counseling psychologist with expertise in separated parenting. (S)he may also be able to help you develop some useful strategies that will help

Q: Is it normal to have both directing affairs in the same area of family activity?

A: It probably isn't normal in the sense that division of domestic areas often falls into naturally efficient departments, presuming that parents mostly respect the way the other does things. They share suggestions and offer back-up support. Separation can mean that because you're parenting on your own, there isn't the scope for undermining one another's methods in front of the children, but you both have lots to offer each other if you communicate about how you manage the various areas of family life.

you manage your feelings and discuss things sensibly with your ex-partner. Do as much reading and consulting and comparing of notes as you can. Then meet again with your ex-partner and readdress the issues.

Make a real commitment

Once you've separated and have initial arrangements in place, stick to the rules. A good divorce is possible and well worth the effort. Like a good marriage, a good divorce takes time and effort. Separated parents need to make sure they conduct themselves with decency and fairness. Keep a record of things that concern you about what everyone is doing and saying. Some of it will be of small long-term consequence, but your journal entries will give you an immediate outlet for inevitable frustrations, as well as providing useful data for your reviews. Meeting regularly to compare notes and discuss the kids is great, and for many it comes naturally. But if you can't do this, it's not crucial. You can co-parent on minimal communication, as we saw when considering parallel parenting.

It was harder in the beginning with all the emotion around
the separation. But we have improved and now sometimes
talk by phone or in person. Email works best for us. We
don't talk a lot now the kids are older. They tend to look
after themselves. —*Arthur*

Communicating and job-sharing

It can help communication to think of shared parenting as being like
job-sharing in the workplace. When you change shifts, you wouldn't
dream of telling your colleague (who, like you, is fully qualified to
do the work) how to do the job you share. But you would tell him
or her relevant information about what had happened during your
shift. And you'd have no trouble deciding what was relevant and
what wasn't, what you thought was worth trying and, having taken
the decision during your shift to deal with something a certain way,
you'd say what follow-through you recommend regardless of how
the other person felt about what you'd started. There's a world of
difference between being concerned enough to offer useful information about what's happened during your children's time with
you, and being interfering, over-intrusive, or insultingly directive.

You can say what happened, what you did, whether it worked,
and what didn't seem to work. The closest you should go to directing or insisting how you want something handled is a warmly
expressed, "I'd really like it if you'd . . ." If you're on the receiving
end, agree to do it if you intend to do it; and if you don't, just say
something like, "Thanks, I'll give that some thought" or "Sure, I
get where you're coming from on that . . ." Suppose, for instance,
that your ex-partner tells you that your son had a nightmare last
night so he may be tired or that your daughter had to see the doctor,
this is what was advised, and asks you to see it through. Even if you
think your ex is a health freak and you disagree with the treatment,
it's unlikely to harm your child, and it's an opportunity to be supportive and cooperative. Your ex will probably ask your daughter

Q: What's the best way to handle things that your child says (s)he is allowed to do by your ex but that you absolutely disapprove of? Is it okay to say you don't care about your ex's wishes?

A: There's always a fine line between reinforcing, for your child's sake, your ex's way of doing things and appearing disinterested so as to prevent yourself as coming across as judgmental! Try to keep a lighthearted, conversational interest in what your ex is saying but don't engage in what you feel about it. Just get on with doing things your way when you're in charge. If you and your ex get on fairly well, you could bring up the next time you are discussing the children—using a neutral, informative tone—why you disapprove of the issue in question, and hope he or she takes it in.

whether you did it and it will go a long way toward goodwill if she can say that you followed through.

Communication methods

1. Talking face to face about the children is ideal.

2. Having a private phone conversation just before changeover can be helpful; but when you're busy, when handovers don't happen directly, or when there's tension, then other methods may work better. Phone calls also have the disadvantage that they can catch someone at a bad moment. In addition, messages left on a machine can be heard by everyone in the room, reducing privacy.

3. Some parents use a kind of logbook that helps both to remember things, and you can make entries as things occur, not

just at the last minute before changeover. Logbooks are best not left in kids' bags for general reading. You should pass it back and forth between the two of you and not use the children as couriers.

4. Email, of course, is very handy. You have a permanent record and can transmit instantly regardless of whether your ex-partner is available. But the written word has some hazards. Your intentions can be misinterpreted when you don't get tone of voice or body language. We tend to write concisely and the printed word can sometimes easily be perceived as cryptic, abrasive, directive, or over-formal, creating misunderstandings.

5. Faxing, though rapidly becoming yesterday's technology, can be useful in the same way as email, with the same advantages and disadvantages.

Sometimes I'd be ready to tear my hair out at the frustrations of trying to talk sensibly together! We both care about the children enormously, but we just can't seem to have a conversation! We've agreed to keep our exchanges to an absolute minimum and use email for the time being. —*Sarah*

Reviews

You'll notice in our sample parenting plans that there are often review clauses. Once you have an agreed plan in place, you should always be open-minded about change, as these are plans about children who are growing and changing all the time—as are their circumstances, just like yours. A plan you've agreed upon, however, should be committed to with all its rules and undertakings for a reasonable amount of time. Reviews should be carried out at least every six months, and not just because a problem seems to have arisen. This is proactive parenting, and it helps you anticipate possible challenges and avert unnecessary complications. And your children will know their parents are getting together regularly to discuss them. With older children, you can involve them in family reviews where everybody can have their say, keeping in mind our advice in Chapters 4 and 6 about involving children in decision making without abdicating parental care and authority.

> Don't ever say, "If it's okay with your father it's okay with me." This places an obligation on the child to check it out with the other parent, and if that parent decides it's *not* okay, then he (or she) is seen in a bad light. Check it out with him yourself if you think it's necessary, and then make your own decision. The kids can accept differences—it just means that Mom and Dad love them in different ways. —*Eileen*

Between you and your children

Many parents feel quite lost without touching base several times a day with their kids because they're used to feeling in touch, and this is the family's style. But shared parenting means you may have to review this. Think carefully: in this age of mobile phones and instant access, what purpose is constant contact really serving? Do you need to keep reassuring yourself, or making sure they're all right? Quite often the phone seems to become a bone of contention, with parents accusing each other of discouraging phone calls between children and the parent they're not with. Children naturally tend to deal with their two-home situation by keeping them separate, and they may not benefit from too much overlap. Respecting the emotional boundaries that usefully exist between the households is important (see also Chapter 4). You are hoping to bring up emotionally independent children, after all. They aren't going to forget you while you're getting on with your life without them. If your relationship with your ex-partner and co-parent is often tense and hostile, and you have a parallel parenting arrangement, then we recommend minimum overlap between households.

When I first heard about Mike's girlfriend, I was worried about how the children were going to feel. They said a few odd things about her that made me wonder what she was really like. But I managed to resist the temptation to talk about her too curiously. They soon seemed to take her for granted, and I guess it was just a matter of getting used to their dad moving on from me a step further. —*Amy*

Why are you calling?

Try asking yourself these questions, and your answers should help you pitch your contact right:

- Am I checking up on whether they're okay? Who is this going to help?
- Do I need to reassure myself they haven't forgotten me?
- Could they feel uncomfortable talking to me when they're over there? Will it help them if I insist?
- Am I afraid of them not needing me?
- If they seem to be calling me over an issue my ex-partner should be dealing with, does it really help if I get involved? Might I unintentionally erode my ex's authority and competence?

Ideally, children should feel free to call sometimes with exciting news, a goodnight message, or a homework problem they know the other parent is good at; and they should be encouraged by the parent they're with to feel free to do so. But they shouldn't be calling because they've been made to feel they must reassure this parent that they're okay, or if they're worried that the parent is okay without them. If you receive calls and you think your children are troubled, reassure them in a way that transmits your confidence in their ability to manage until you next see them, and encourage your ex-partner to deal with these little uncertainties themselves. Saying things at drop-off like, "Don't worry, I'll have the phone on all the time if you need me" or "If you're upset, just call and I'll come and pick you up," or even "I'll miss you" tends to transmit uncertainty and will contribute to children's own anxieties. This is setting them up to feel uncomfortable and insecure, and implies that the other parent might not look after them properly. This is a burden that they—and the other parent—just do not need.

> I thought it was really important for the kids to know I was thinking of them, so I always rang them to say goodnight. —*Alex*

Managing pick-ups and drop-offs

Communication during transition times is especially important, because changing from one parent to the other is often quite hard for children. If everything is going smoothly and you parents are friendly with one another, then lingering during the changeovers is fine, sending a positive message about parental cooperation. If not, keep them brief. Cultivating your children's independence by having them run out to greet the other parent shows you're confident in them and keeps uneasy parents apart. Even when there isn't tension between parents, it can be helpful for the children if you see them to school at the end of your shift and have them go from school straight to their other home, even if some of their belongings have to go separately. This arrangement gives them six hours of emotionally neutral time as a kind of buffer between their two worlds, making the transition easier. Sometimes pick-ups and drop-offs can be done more smoothly through a third party such as a grandparent.

* * * * *

Michael says: Sometimes it helps, especially when you find it difficult or impossible to talk sensibly to your ex-partner, to look at your separation/divorce as a business. The nature of the business is parenting your children. The end products are healthy and happy children, growing into independent good citizens. The means of production are your parenting plan and the activities and attitudes that you put into it. You are both partners in the business of raising your children.

Jill says: Some parents worry about who should attend what school functions or whether both parents should always try to go. Both of you going and being together for them helps, but not if it generates tension that the children pick up. There may be sensitivities about new partners' involvement, too. Family occasions where you are together as a unit despite your separation shouldn't be avoided for fear of confusing the children. Such occasions show that you are still a family so far as their welfare and heritage are concerned. There's always a compromise possible!

• • • • •

KEY MESSAGES

- Carefully plan difficult discussions with your ex-partner.
- It is crucial for co-parents to communicate constructively.
- It is important to commit to your parenting plan, but sometimes a review is necessary.
- Think of shared parenting as job-sharing.
- How you communicate can have different impacts.
- Don't contact your children excessively when they are with your ex-partner.
- Changeovers can be tricky.

Authors' notes

PAGE 4   "Studies over the years have consistently shown that the worst part of divorce for children is the loss of one parent."

J. B. Kelly, "Developing Beneficial Parenting Plan Models for Children Following Separation and Divorce," *Journal of the American Academy of Matrimonial Lawyers* 19 (2005): pp. 237–254.

PAGE 9   "Research on the outcomes for children of divorce has produced varied results. However, there is agreement that separation can put children at serious risk in a number of ways."

B. Rodgers and J. Prior, *Divorce and Separation: The Outcomes for Children* (York: Joseph Rowntree Foundation, 1998).

J. S. Wallerstein, J. M. Lewis, and S. Blakeslee, *The Unexpected Legacy of Divorce: The 25-year Landmark Study* (New York: Hyperion, 2000).

E. N. Hetherington and J. Kelly, *For Better or Worse: Divorce Reconsidered* (New York: Norton & Co, 2002).

PAGE 9   "Currently about 80 percent of the children whose parents are separated live in sole-mother custody arrangements, and as many as a third of them have little or no contact with their fathers."

Australian Bureau of Statistics, "Family Characteristics Survey 1997," Catalogue No 4442.0 ABS, Canberra.

Office of National Statistics, "Population Trends 1987" (UK, 1998).

J. Bradshaw, C. Stimson, J. Williams, and C. Skinner, *Absent Fathers?* (London: Routledge, 1999).

L. Trinder, M. Beek, and J. Connolly, *Making Contact: How Parents and Children Negotiate and Experience Contact after Divorce* (York: YPS in association with Joseph Rowntree Foundation, 2002).

PAGE 9   "The common arrangement for parenting children after divorce—living with Mom and visiting Dad—often leaves everyone dissatisfied."

W. V. Fabricius and J. A. Hall, "Young Adults' Perspectives on Divorce: Living Arrangements," *Family & Conciliation Courts Review* 38 (2000): pp. 446–461.

C. Smart, B. Neale, and A. Wade, *The Changing Experience of Childhood: Families and Divorce* (Cambridge: Polity Press, 2001).

J. Hunt, *Researching Contact* (London: National Council for One-Parent Families, 2003).

Bruce Smyth (ed), *Research Report No. 9* (Australian Institute of Family Studies, 2004).

L. Laumann-Billings and R. E. Emery, "Distress among Young Adults from Divorced Families," *Journal of Family Psychology* 14 (2000): pp. 671–687.

D. Blankenhorn, *Fatherless America: Confronting Our Most Urgent Social Problem* (New York: Basic Books, 1995).

E. Kruk, *Divorce and Disengagement: Patterns of Fatherhood within and beyond Marriage* (Halifax: Fernwood Publications, 1993).

G. Greif, "When Divorced Fathers Want No Contact with Their Children: A Preliminary Analysis," *Journal of Divorce and Remarriage* 23 (1995): pp. 75–84.

PAGE 10   "There is evidence that it does little for solid parent–child
relationships, and can reduce one parent to onlooker
status."

L. Laumann-Billings and R. E. Emery, "Distress Among
Young Adults from Divorced Families," *Journal of Family
Psychology* 14 (2000): pp. 671–687.

A. Ferro, "'Standard' Contact in Parent–Child Contact
and Post-Separation Arrangements," *Research Report
No. 9* (Australian Institute of Family Studies, 2004).

A. Hillery, "The Case for Joint Custody," *The Best Parent
Is Both Parents* (Norfolk, VA: Hampton Roads Publishing, 1993).

M. Roman and W. Haddad, "The Case for Joint Custody,"
Psychology Today September (1978): pp. 196–205.

J. B. Kelly, "Developing Beneficial Parenting Plan Models
for Children Following Separation and Divorce," *Journal
of the American Academy of Matrimonial Lawyers* 19
(2005): pp. 237–254.

PAGE 10   "[C]hildren in shared-care arrangements are more satisfied
and appear to be better adjusted."

J. Kelly, "Longer-Term Adjustment in Children of Divorce,"
Journal of Family Psychology 2 (1988): pp. 119–140.

R. Bauserman, "Child Adjustment in Joint Custody Versus
Sole-Custody Arrangements: A Meta-Analytic Review,"
Journal of Family Psychology 16 (2002): pp. 91–102.

J. B. Mosten, "Dual Household Joint Custody and
Adolescent Separation-Individuation," *Dissertation for the
Faculty of California Graduate Institute* (July 2002).

PAGE 10   "Because families are all so different, no one post-divorce
arrangement can be said to be in the best interests of all
children."

D. N. Lye, *The Washington State Parenting Plan Study:
Report to the Washington State Gender and Justice Com-
mission and Domestic Relations Commission* (Washington:
Washington State Courts, 1999).

M. A. Mason, *The Custody Wars* (New York: Basic Books, 2000).

I. Ricci, *Mom's House, Dad's House: Making Two Homes for Your Child* (New York: Simon and Schuster, 1997).

J. S. Wallerstein and S. Blakeslee, *What About the Kids? Raising Your Children before, during and after Divorce* (New York: Hyperion, 2003).

PAGE 11   "Your children need time with both of their parents, time that is meaningful."

K. Funder, *Remaking Families* (Melbourne: AIFS, 1996).

E. E. Maccoby, R. H. Mnookin, et al., "Private Ordering Revisited: What Custodial Arrangements Are Parents Negotiating?" *Divorce Reform at the Crossroads* (New Haven, CT: Yale University Press, 1990).

J. S. Wallerstein and S. Blakeslee, *What About the Kids?* (New York: Hyperion, 2003).

J. Pryor and B. Rogers, *Children in Changing Families: Life after Parental Separation* (Oxford: Blackwell, 2001).

B. Smyth, C. Caruana, and A. Ferro, *Some Whens, Hows, and Whys of Shared Care: What Separated Parents Who Spend Equal Time with Their Children Say about Shared Parenting* (Australian Social Policy Conference, 2003).

PAGE 11   "Shared parenting can produce happier children and more satisfied parents."

P. Parkinson and B. Smyth, "When the Difference Is Night and Day: Some Empirical Insights into Patterns of Parent–Child Contact after Separation," Paper presented at the 8th Australian Institute of Family Studies Conference, Melbourne (2003).

B. Smyth, G. Sheehan, and B. Fehlberg, "Patterns of Parenting after Divorce: A Pre-Reform Act Benchmark Study," *Australian Journal of Family Law* 15 (2001): pp. 114–128.

B. Smyth and R. Weston, "Attitudes to 50/50 shared care in Australia," *Family Matters* 63 (2004): pp. 54–59.

B Öberg and G. Öberg, *Den Delade Familjen* (Stockholm: Department of Education, Stockholm University, 1985).

J. Kelly, "Longer Term Adjustment in Children of Divorce," *Journal of Family Psychology* 2 (1988): pp. 119–140.

R. Bauserman, "Child Adjustment in Joint Custody Versus Sole-Custody Arrangements: A Meta-Analytic Review," *Journal of Family Psychology* 16 (2002): pp. 91–102.

P. R. Amato and J. G. Gilbreth, "Nonresidential Fathers and Children's Well-Being: A Meta-Analysis," *Journal of Marriage and the Family* 61 (1999): pp. 557–573.

J. Dunn, "Contact and Children's Perspectives on Parental Relationships," *Children and Their Families: Contact, Rights and Welfare* (Oxford: Hart Publishing, 2003).

PAGE 16   "Mediation, conflict resolution programs, and counseling have been shown to be successful in assisting separated parents to develop the attitudes and skills that enable them to become cooperative parents."

J. B. Kelly, "Further Observations on Joint Custody," *University of California Davis Law Review* 16, p. 762.

R. Neff and K. Cooper, "Parental Conflict Resolution: Six-, Twelve- and Fifteen-Month Follow-ups of a High Conflict Program," *Family Court Review* 42 (2004): pp. 99–114.

B. McKenzie and I. Guberman, "For the Sake of the Children: A Parent Education Program for Separating and Divorcing Parents" (Winnipeg: University of Manitoba, 2000).

B. L. Bacon and B. McKenzie, "Parent Education after Separation/Divorce: Impact of the Level of Parental Conflict on Outcomes," *Family Court Review* 42 (2004): pp. 85–98.

PAGE 18   "There is reliable evidence that parents who have good relationships with their children pay more child support."

B. Smyth (ed), *Research Report No. 9* (Australian Institute of Family Studies, 2004).

G. Davis and N. Wikely, "National Survey of Child Support Agency Clients—the Relationship Dimension," *Family Law* 32 (2002): pp. 522–527.

J. Bradshaw et al., *Absent Fathers?* (London: Routledge, 1999).

PAGE 20   "All the research indicates that children hunger for the love and attention of their fathers and are deeply affected when they don't get it."

P. M. Stahl, "A Review of Joint and Shared Parenting Literature," *Joint Custody and Shared Parenting,* Washington DC Bureau of National Affairs, Association of Family and Conciliation Courts.

J. Wallerstein and J. Kelly, *Surviving the Break-Up—How Children and Parents Cope with Divorce* (London: Grant McIntyre, 1980).

P. R. Amato, "Children of Divorce in the 1990s: An Update of the Amato and Keith 1991 Meta-Analysis," *Journal of Family Psychology* 15 (2001): pp. 355–370.

PAGE 22   "If a father is discouraged from remaining or becoming involved, there are other consequences for mother, father and children."

P. M. Stahl, "A Review of Joint and Shared Parenting Literature," *Joint Custody and Shared Parenting*, Washington DC Bureau of National Affairs, Association of Family and Conciliation Courts.

J. Wallerstein and J. Kelly, *Surviving the Break-Up—How Children and Parents Cope with Divorce* (London: Grant McIntyre, 1980).

P. R. Amato, "Children of Divorce in the 1990s: An Update of the Amato and Keith 1991 Meta-Analysis," *Journal of Family Psychology* 15 (2001): pp. 355–370.

PAGE 22   "Mothers with shared parenting may be less stressed and therefore better parents and workers."

B. Smyth (ed), *Research Report No. 9* (Australian Institute of Family Studies, 2004).

PAGE 28   "Research shows that the children who adjust best are the ones who don't lose a relationship with a parent because of a separation."

J. Pryor and B. Rodgers, *Children in Changing Families: Life after Parental Separation* (Oxford: Blackwell Publishers, 2001).

L. Trinder, M. Beek, and J. Connolly, *Making Contact: How Parents and Children Negotiate and Experience Contact after Divorce* (York: Joseph Rowntree Foundation, 2002).

T. Arendell, *Co-parenting: A review of the literature* (Philadelphia, PA: National Center on Fathers and Families, 1996).

M. Benjamin and H. H. Irving, "Shared Parenting: Critical Review of the Research Literature," *Family and Conciliation Courts Review* 27 (1989): pp. 21–35.

Australian Institute of Family Studies, *Submission of the AIFS to the House of Representatives Standing Committee on Family and Community Affairs Inquiry into Child Custody Arrangements in the Event of Family Separation* (Melbourne: AIFS, 2003).

PAGE 28   "It takes time, availability and repetition to make the bonding strong."

L. Laumann-Billings and R. E. Emery, "Distress among Young Adults from Divorced Families," *Journal of Family Psychology* 14 (2000): pp. 671–687.

A. Ferro, "'Standard' Contact in Parent–Child Contact and Post-Separation Arrangements," *Research Report No. 9* (Australian Institute of Family Studies, 2004).

PAGE 31   "The stability that children need is more than geographical stability. It is emotional stability."

See J. B. Mosten, *Dual Household Joint Custody and Adolescent Separation-Individuation*, Dissertation for the

Faculty of California Graduate Institute (July 2002). This is an important study. The author followed the attitudes and progress of 12 young people over two years, all of them in shared parenting situations. While disliking the hassles of living in two places, the young people were overwhelmingly in favor of shared custody and could not imagine any alternative that would permit the same close relationship with both parents.

PAGE 34   "There is growing evidence that overnight stays in infancy form a meaningful basis for parent–child relations from an early age."

M. K. Pruett, R. Ebling, and G. Isabella, "Critical Aspects of Parenting Plans for Young Children: Injecting Data into the Debate about Overnights," *Family Court Review* 42 (2004): pp. 35–59.

R. Warshak, "Blanket Restrictions: Overnight Contact between Parents and Young Children," *Family and Conciliation Courts Review* 39 (2000): pp. 365–371.

J. B. Kelly "Developing Beneficial Parenting Plan Models for Children Following Separation and Divorce," *Journal of the American Academy of Matrimonial Lawyers* 19 (2005): pp. 237–254.

PAGE 35   "Children need time to do ordinary things with each parent, not just fun things on holidays and weekends."

L. Laumann-Billings and R. E. Emery, "Distress among Young Adults from Divorced Families," *Journal of Family Psychology* 14 (2000): pp. 671–687.

A. Burgess and G. Russell, *Supporting Fathers: Contributions from the International Fatherhood Summit* (The Hague: Bernard van Leer Foundation, 2004) See www .fathersdirect.com/index.php?id=12&cID=78.

PAGE 36   "Authoritative and engaged parenting creates emotional bonding between father and child, which contributes significantly to the child's well-being."

P. R. Amato and J. G. Gilbreth, "Non-Resident Fathers and Children's Wellbeing: A Meta-Analysis," *Journal of Marriage and the Family* 61 (1999): pp. 557–573.

PAGE 37   "But common sense and logic tell us that a close parenting relationship demands lots of time!"

B. Smyth (ed), "Parent–Child Contact and Post-Separation Parenting Arrangements," *Research Report No 9* (Melbourne: Australian Institute of Family Studies, 2004).

PAGE 37   "This conclusion is inconsistent with research, which shows that good contact arrangements result in reduced conflict between parents."

B. Smyth, C. Caruana, and A. Ferro, "Father–Child Contact after Separation: Profiling Five Different Patterns of Care," *Family Matters* (Autumn 2004).

M. K. Pruett and K. Hoganbruen, "Joint Custody and Shared Parenting, Research and Interventions," *Child and Adolescent Psychiatric Clinics of North America* 2 (April 1998).

R. Bauserman, "Child Adjustment in Joint Custody Versus Sole-Custody Arrangements: A Meta-Analytic Review," *Journal of Family Psychology* 16 (2002): pp. 91–102.

PAGE 39   "[C]hildren can cope with this as well as adults."

J. B. Kelly, "Children's Adjustment in Conflicted Marriage and Divorce: A Decade Review of Research," *Journal of American Academy of Child and Adolescent Psychiatry* 39 (August 2002): p. 8.

PAGE 43   "So care needs to be taken in involving children in separation planning."

C. Smart, "From Children's Shoes to Children's Voices," *Family Court Review* 40 (2002): pp. 307–319.

K. Kaltenborn, "Parent–Child Contact after Divorce: The Need to Consider the Child's Perspective," *Marriage and Family Review* 36 (2004): pp. 67–90.

PAGE 43   "A mother and father with different parenting styles can complement one another effectively."

K. D. Pruett, *Fatherneed: Why Father Care Is as Essential as Mothercare for Your Child* (New York: The Free Press, 2000).

PAGE 46   "Litigation exacerbates conflict between parents and increases pressure on children."

S. Zaidel, "Taking Divorce out of the Context of Dispute Resolution," *Family Court Review* 42 (2004): pp. 678–680.

I. Ricci, *Mom's House, Dad's House: Making Two Homes for Your Child* (New York: Simon and Schuster, 1997).

D. A. Luepnitz, *Child Custody: A Study of Families after Divorce* (Lexington, MA: Lexington Books, 1982).

PAGE 46   "Children pick up on continuing parental conflict, and it can have seriously damaging consequences for them."

P. R. Amato and J. G. Gilbreth, "Non-Resident Fathers and Children's Well-Being: A Meta-Analysis," *Journal of Marriage and the Family* 61 (1999): pp. 557–573.

R. Bauserman, "Child Adjustment in Joint Custody Versus Sole-Custody Arrangements: A Meta-Analytic Review," *Journal of Family Psychology* 16 (2002): pp. 91–102.

M.-Y. Lee, "A Model of Children's Post-Divorce Behavioral Adjustment in Maternal and Dual Residence Arrangements," *Journal of Family Issues* 23 (2002): pp. 672–697.

J. Pryor and R. Daly-Peoples, "Adolescent Attitudes toward Living Arrangements after Divorce," *Child and Family Law Quarterly* 13 (2001): pp. 197–208.

P. R. Amato and S. J. Rezac, "Contact with Nonresidential Parents, Interparental Conflict, and Children's Behavior," *Journal of Family Issues* 15 (1994): pp. 191–207.

J. Reynolds (ed), *Not in Front of the Children? How Conflict between Parents Affects Children* (London: One Plus One Marriage and Partnership Research, 2001).

PAGE 48   "Divorce can be a trigger for improved relationships
           between children and parents, especially between children
           and their fathers."

           J. Wallerstein and J. Kelly, *Surviving the Break-Up—How
           Children and Parents Cope with Divorce* (London: Grant
           McIntyre, 1980).

           B. Smyth, C. Caruana, and A. Ferro, *Some Whens, Hows,
           and Whys of Shared Care: What Separated Parents Who
           Spend Equal Time with Their Children Say about Shared
           Parenting* (Australian Social Policy Conference, 2003).

PAGE 53   "As we noted in Chapter 2, recent research into shared
           parenting suggests that it works for kids if it's managed in
           a child-focused way but not if it's managed in a competi-
           tive, adult-focused way."

           B. Neale, J. Flowerdew, and C. Smart, "Drifting Towards
           Shared Residence? Report from Centre for Research on
           Family, Kinship, and Childhood (Leeds)," *Family Law*
           (December 2003): pp. 904–908.

           H. H. Irving and M. Benjamin, "Shared Parenting:
           Critical Review of The Research Literature," *Family and
           Conciliation Courts Review* 27 (1989): pp. 21–35.

PAGE 67   "[T]here are good reasons why care needs to be taken here."

           C. Smart, "From Children's Shoes to Children's Voices,"
           Family Court Review 40 (2002): pp. 307–319.

           K. Kaltenborn, "Parent–Child Contact after Divorce: The
           Need to Consider the Child's Perspective," *Marriage and
           Family Review* 36 (2004): pp. 67–90.

PAGE 71   "Our experience tells us—and studies in the United States
           confirm it— that children, as well as adults, benefit from
           programs that help them cope with the changes in their
           lives due to their parents' separation."

           J. Pedro-Carroll, "Fostering Resilience in the Aftermath
           of Divorce: The Role of Evidence-Based Programs for
           Children," *Family Court Review* 43 (2005): pp. 52–64.

S. A. Wolchik et al., "Programs for Promoting Parenting of Residential Parents: Moving from Efficacy to Effectiveness," *Family Court Review* 43 (2005): pp. 65–80.

PAGE 78 "Even very young children can benefit from overnight stays with another parent."

J. B. Kelly and M. E. Lamb, "Using Child Development Research to Make Appropriate Custody and Access Decisions for Young Children," *Family and Conciliation Courts Review* 38 (2000): pp. 297–311.

M. E. Lamb and J. B. Kelly, "Using the Empirical Literature to Guide the Development of Parenting Plans for Young Children," *Family Court Review* 39 (2001) pp. 365–371.

R. Warshak, "Blanket Restrictions: Overnight Contact between Parents and Young Children," *Family and Conciliation Courts Review* 38 (2000): pp. 422–445.

PAGE 90 "For parents who find it impossible to get along, parallel parenting can work."

B. Smyth, C. Caruana, and A. Ferro, "Father–Child Contact after Separation: Profiling Five Different Patterns of Care," *Family Matters* 67 (Autumn 2004).

I. Ricci, *Mom's House, Dad's House: Making Two Homes for Your Children* (New York: Simon & Schuster, 1997).

F. F. Furstenberg Jr. and A. J. Cherlin, *Divided Families: What Happens to Children when Parents Part* (Cambridge, MA: Harvard University Press, 1991).

Acknowledgments

The authors send warm thanks and appreciation to the many mothers, fathers, sons, and daughters who were willing to share their experiences of life after divorce and separation. Through their generosity, this book rests securely on real life as well as on academic research.

The authors are also most grateful for the contributions of Jody Mosten, PhD, Richard Warshak, PhD, Sanford Braver, PhD, and Marsha Kline Pruett, PhD in assisting us to prepare this edition of the book for North American readers. Their expertise and advice, together with their work in this area, are recognized and greatly appreciated.

Helpful resources

Most people need help through and in the aftermath of separation and divorce. Our experience is that this help is found with good divorce counselors, quality mediators, and sensible lawyers.

We also recommend post-separation parenting courses. There is overwhelming evidence that intensive programs—as opposed to information sessions—can change both attitudes and behavior, and lead to better parenting of children in separated families. Such programs can be accessed through the family courts, community welfare organizations, and separation counselors. Many can be found on the Internet.

Recommended reading

Ahrons, Constance R. *The Good Divorce*. New York: Bloomsbury, 1995.

Balson, Maurice. *Becoming Better Parents*. Melbourne: Australian Council for Educational Research, 1991.

Biddulph, Steve. *Raising Boys*. 2nd ed. Sydney: Finch Publishing, 2003.

———. *The Secret of Happy Children*. Sydney: Harper Collins, 1994.

Brooks, Robert, and Sam Goldstein. *Raising Resilient Children: Fostering Strength, Hope, and Optimism in Your Child*. New York: Contemporary Books, McGraw-Hill, 2001.

Burrett, Jill. *Dad's Place: A New Guide for Fathers after Divorce*. Sydney: Carrington Psychology, 2001.

———. *Parenting after Separation: Making the Most of Family Changes*. Sydney: Finch, 2002.

Emery, Robert E. *The Truth about Children and Divorce: Dealing with the Emotions so You and Your Children Can Thrive*. New York: Penguin, 2004.

Folberg, Jay (ed). *Joint Custody and Shared Parenting*. 2nd ed. New York: Guilford Press, 1991.

Galper, Miriam. *Co-Parenting: Sharing Your Children Equally*. Philadelphia: Running Press, 1978.

Gordon, Dr. Thomas. *Parent Effectiveness Training*. New York: Three Rivers Press, 2000.

Gottman, John. *The Heart of Parenting: How to Raise an Emotionally Intelligent Child*. London: Bloomsbury, 1997.

Green, Dr. Christopher. *Beyond Toddlerdom: Keeping Five- to Twelve-Year-Olds on the Rail*. Sydney: Doubleday, 2000.

Planning for Shared Parenting: A Guide for Parents Living Apart. Madison, WI: AFCC Publications.

Ricci, Isolina. *Mom's House, Dad's House: A Complete Guide for Parents Who Are Separated, Divorced or Remarried*. Madison, WI: AFCC Publications, 1997.

Sanders, Matthew R. *Every Parent: A Positive Approach to Children's Behavior*. Melbourne: Penguin, 2004.

Warshak, Richard A. *Divorce Poison: Protecting the Parent–Child Bond from a Vindictive Ex*. New York: Harper Paperbacks, 2003.

Index

About the authors

Jill Burrett is a consulting psychologist with more than 30 years of experience helping parents and families to manage challenging family changes. In 1988 she created Carrington Psychology, which offers consulting, assessment, counseling, and mediation services. Her interest in helping ease family separations began with her years in the Family Court of Australia at Sydney where she directed the rapidly developing counseling and mediation services during the early 1980s.

She has published academic and professional articles, relationship and parenting pieces for magazines, and five books on relationships and separated parenting topics, including *Parenting after Separation: Making the Most of Family Changes*.

Jill holds a Masters of Science degree in Child Development and Educational Psychology from London University. She is the mother of two young adults and the stepmother of her partner's first son.

Michael Green became a lawyer in 1975 and started his legal career in private practice, mainly in civil and criminal law. He began working in the Family Court of Australia soon after it was created and became a Queens Counsel in 1988. When he returned to private practice in 1996, Michael appeared before appellate courts and the High Court of Australia. In 2000, Michael retired from the bar to further his interest in mediation and family relationships.

His private mediation practice addresses issues related to separation: parenting, living arrangements, child support, property division, and more. In addition to mediation, he offers coaching for those going through separation.

Author of *Fathers after Divorce: Building a New Life and Becoming a Successful Separated Parent,* Michael has long been interested in parenting issues. As a former president of the Shared Parenting Council of Australia, he participated in the federal government's consultations which resulted in extensive reforms to Australian family law.